THE SHAMBHALA ANTHOLOGY OF WOMEN'S SPIRITUAL POETRY

OTHER BOOKS BY ALIKI BARNSTONE

POETRY

The Real Tin Flower

Windows in Providence

Madly in Love

ANTHOLOGIES

A Book of Women Poets from Antiquity to Now
with Willis Barnstone

The Calvinist Roots of the Modern Era
with Michael Tomasek Manson and Carol J. Singley

EDITION

Trilogy by H.D.
Introduction and Readers' Notes by Aliki Barnstone

The Shambhala Anthology
OF WOMEN'S SPIRITUAL POETRY

Edited by
ALIKI BARNSTONE

SHAMBHALA
Boston & London
2002

SHAMBHALA PUBLICATIONS, INC.
Horticultural Hall
300 Massachusetts Avenue
Boston, Massachusetts 02115
www.shambhala.com

9 8 7 6 5 4 3 2 1

FIRST PAPERBACK EDITION
Printed in the United States of America

⊗ This edition is printed on acid-free paper that meets
the American National Standards Institute z39.48 Standard.
Distributed in the United States by Random House, Inc.,
and in Canada by Random House of Canada Ltd

LIBRARY OF CONGRESS CATALOGING-IN-PUBLICATION DATA
Voices of light.
The Shambhala anthology of women's spiritual poetry/
edited by Aliki Barnstone.
p. cm.
ISBN 1-57062-975-7
1. Poetry—Collections. 2. Poetry—Women authors.
3. Spiritual life—Poetry.
I. Barnstone, Aliki. II. Title.
PN6109.9.V65 2002
808.81'0082—DC21
2002070575

For the Greek spirit in

my grandmother
MARIKA TZALOPOULOU (1900–1995)

my mother
ELLI TZALOPOULOU BARNSTONE

and my daughter
ZOË MARIKA BARNSTONE-CLARK

From the doorsill of heaven comes the word:
"Welcome!"

—ENHEDUANNA

Why—do they shut Me out of Heaven?
Did I sing—too loud?

—EMILY DICKINSON

CONTENTS

PREFACE

This book contains spiritual and visionary poetry by women—from the ancient Sumerian moon priestess Enheduanna to poets living among us now. In most cultures women have not often been in positions of religious authority. Yet, as outsiders—whether living as Buddhist nuns in Tibet or in the forests of Nepal; living in convents of Spain, Italy, Germany, or Holland; or writing in Calvinist New England—these spiritual dissidents found their own direct, sometimes heretical, ways to envision the sacred. And they named those ways in verse. Though often deprived of public position, women have always practiced the personal art of writing and so have been prepared to be our spiritual and visionary voices of light.

Though most of the women poets in this book lived in subordinate circumstances, there are a few notable exceptions. As a moon priestess and daughter of the king of Sumeria, Enheduanna *was* in a position of religious authority. And because she was a spiritual leader forty-three hundred years ago, her work was preserved on cuneiform tablets—the oldest known poetic writing. She is now the first writer known to the world. As poet and priestess, Enheduanna felt esteemed and powerful enough to write: "From the doorsill of heaven comes the word: / 'Welcome!' " In contrast to Enheduanna is Emily Dickinson, who wrote in solitude in Amherst, Massachusetts: "Why—do they shut Me out of Heaven? / Did I sing—too loud?" In bringing together these and the other spiritual poems by women collected here, I have wished to allow these poets to sing loud, whether or not they were welcomed by the heavens or their own social situations, whether they are remembered or largely forgotten.

The spiritual impulse sparks a visionary quest toward self-realization. That quest is usually expressed as a desire for union with nature or a godhead, with a secular or divine lover, with the principle of light, or with the "word." The word may be God's sent word or the ecstatic, visionary experience of writing a poem. Some mystical poets seek a spiritual union in death—a death of being either outside time and space in a flash of eternity or in an afterlife. Death is, in Dickinson's words, the "most profound experiment / Appointed unto Men—." The women poets gathered together in these pages write out of diverse spiritual traditions, yet they share an experience of the self uniting with an outside force through an inner vision. Sappho writes of this spiritual desire for union:

> I could not hope
> to touch the sky
> with my two arms.

Though she claims she could not hope, her words, paradoxically, express a fervent hope that her united soul and body might reach out to embrace the sky and Aphrodite—and make immensity personal, intimate, and transcendent.

Many of the poems in this book are love poems, sometimes overtly erotic ones. These poems are spiritual in the sense that they explore erotic union that is divine and ecstatic. An essential example is the biblical Song of Songs. To justify its inclusion in the Hebrew Bible, Jewish scholars have interpreted it as a spiritual allegory celebrating the marriage of Israel to Yahweh, and Christian interpreters view it as an allegory for the marriage of the church to Christ. For the mystic poets, the Song of Songs represents the loving union between the soul (always as the female speaker) and God. We see this view in many poetic retellings of the Song of Songs, from early Kabbalah to sixteenth-century Saint John of the Cross's mystico-erotic "Dark Night of the Soul" and "Spiritual Canticle." The Song of Songs is the ultimate union of love and spirit and, as such, has been the world's love song of love songs.

Many of the poems collected here addressed to deities are luminously erotic, especially those by the Indian poets Mirabai and Mahadevi, and the Sufi mystics Rabia and Bibi Hayati. Some are even humorous, as in the mocking anonymous poems from the *Gatha Saptashati*:

> Clearly a god is kissing that lady,
> making her nipples go stiff.
> There is no way to approve of such a lover,
> even if he is a god.

Other poets seek spiritual union with nature. Classical Chinese poetry equates nature with the spirit in parallelistic verses: the first line depicts nature; the second the human response to it. In one of my favorite poems the Tang poet Yu Xuanji writes in "For Hidden Mist Pavilion":

Spring flowers and autumn moon enter poems.
Bright days and clear nights are fit for idle gods.

Raised in vain the pearl screen, never lowered.
Long ago, I moved my couch to face the mountain.

The poet attains union with the spring flowers and autumn moon that
have entered her poems, along with the bright days and clear nights.
The human response to nature is conveyed by Yu's moving her couch to
face and meditate upon the mountain and join her yearning spirit with
nature.

H.D., Carolyn Forché, Ruth Stone, Marina Tsvetayeva, and others
look for spiritual fusion with people. Theirs is a "poetry of witness" that
reminds us that the spirit is within everyone and unites us through em-
pathy with the suffering (personal or political) or the joy of each person.
H.D. wrote *Trilogy* during World War II as an antiwar work. She calls
for what she names "spiritual realism," arguing against a utilitarian
viewpoint that would justify the atrocity of war and dismiss the power
of the spirit and of love. She asks "after the bitter fire of destruction"
that we

leave the smoldering cities below
(we have done all we could),

we have given until we have no more to give;
alas, it was pity, rather than love, we gave;

now having given all, let us leave all,
above all, let us leave pity

and mount higher
to love—resurrection.

Pity is not emphatic, for it involves distancing oneself from the person
suffering. So H.D. exhorts us to "mount higher / to love," which is more
painful but closes distances between us.

Death and self-annihilation also have powerful spiritual significance.
Some poets, such as Anne Bradstreet, look forward to the afterlife,
when they will meet God and be reunited with their dead loved ones.
Bradstreet at once blames God and ambivalently praises him for the
tragic loss of her grandchildren. "The heavens have changed to sorrow
my delight." Yet she chides herself for mourning because the Puritans

believed it wrong to grieve too much, to "love the creation more than the Creator":

> More fool than I to look on that was lent,
> As if mine own, when thus impermanent.
> Farewell dear child, thou ne're shall come to me,
> But yet a while, and I shall go to thee;
> Mean time my throbbing heart's cheered up with this:
> Thou with my Saviour art in endless bliss.

As a Buddhist would speak of the impermanence of human life, Bradstreet, waiting for reunion after life, states that she loved her granddaughter "that was lent, / As if mine own, when thus impermanent."

Most religious traditions, Eastern and Western, advocate a death of the self in order to unite with the godhead or with the cosmos. In the following anonymous Sanskrit song the speaker imagines herself becoming one with the lover-god by "vanishing into him":

> When he comes back
> to my arms
>
> I'll make him feel
> what nobody ever felt
>
> everywhere
> me
> vanishing into him
>
> like water
> into the clay of a new jar.

By a mystical erotic act of self-annihilation the lover merges totally with the deity, is "everywhere," and thereby merges with the creation. In her poem "Wake" Tess Gallagher inverts the idea that loved ones will reunite in the afterlife, uniting with her dead lover while she is still alive. Like the Sanskrit poet, the speaker has a few moments of becoming dead and vanishing into her husband's death. She climbs into bed with her beloved and for a while "wakes dead" with him:

> We were dead
> a little while together then, serene

and afloat on the strange broad canopy
of the abandoned world.

Poets as diverse in religious tradition and era as the Calvinist Emily
Dickinson (1830–1886) and the Hindu Muktabai (thirteenth century)
carry the death of the self into the creation of words and art: the self
must be annihilated, the "senses end," and ordinary consciousness
transformed into ecstatic consciousness. Mukta Bai writes:

Though he has no form
my eyes saw him,

his glory is fire in my mind
that knows

his secret inner form
invented by the soul

What is
beyond the mind

has no boundary.
In it our senses end.

Mukta says: Words cannot hold him
yet in him all words are.

When the fire burns the mind, the soul invents a divine secret form,
beyond boundary, where all words originate, inadequate though they
are. "Words cannot hold him," the poet acknowledges, while simultane-
ously holding him in the words of her poem, naming herself ("Mukta
says") and claiming the poem as her own.
    Dickinson similarly engages in self-annihilation that results in poetic
re-creation or rebirth:

Me from Myself—to banish—
Had I Art—
Impregnable my Fortress
Unto All Heart—

But since Myself—assault Me—
How have I peace

Except by subjugating
Consciousness?

And since We're mutual Monarch
How this be
Except by Abdication—
Me—of Me?

In this poem, which is characteristically tormented, witty, and ironic, the speaker sees that she can have peace only by "subjugating / Consciousness," by separating the worldly self from the spiritual self. The poet seeks the kind of self-abdication that a Calvinist would hope for in order to be reborn in Christ. In the process the poem reveals the impossibility of such a self-banishment and the words on the page leave the traces of the self's assault on itself. Both Mukta Bai and Emily Dickinson venture where the "senses end," where the self burns away, and they return with poetry.

The act of writing poetry is itself visionary and spiritual, for it requires an ecstatic state, a moment elsewhere, a re-creation of the self, and a quest for words to unite with the reader, whether that reader is the Creator—or you.

The Shambhala Anthology of Women's Spiritual Poetry

ENHEDUANNA

(CA. 2300 BCE)

Inanna and the Holy Light

You with your voices of light,
Lady of all the essences
whom heaven and earth love,
temple friend of An,
you wear immense ornaments,
you desire the tiara of the high priestess
whose hand holds the seven essences.
O my lady, guardian of all the great essences,
you have picked them up and hang them
over your fingers.
You gather the holy essences and wear them
tightly on your breasts.

Moon Goddess Inanna and An

Like a dragon you fill the land with venom.
Like thunder when you roar over the earth,
trees and plants fall before you.
You are a flood descending from a mountain,
O first one,
moon goddess Inanna of heaven and earth!
Your fire blows about and drops on our nation.
Lady mounted on a beast,
An gives you qualities, holy commands,
and you decide.
You are in all our great rites.
Who can understand you?

Inanna and Enlil

Storms lend you wings, destroyer of the lands.
Loved by Enlil, you fly over our nation.
You serve the decrees of An.
O my lady, on hearing your sound,
hills and flatlands bow.
When we come before you, terrified,
shuddering in your stormy clear light,
we receive justice.
We sing, mourn, and cry before you,
and walk toward you along a path
from the house of enormous sighs.

Inanna and Ebih

In the mountains where you are not worshiped
the vegetation is cursed.
You turn its grand entrance into ashes,
rivers soar high with blood
and the people have nothing to drink.
The army of the mountains comes to you captive
of its own accord.
Healthy young men parade before you
of their own accord.
The dancing city is filled with storm,
driving young men to you as your captives.

Banishment from Ur

You asked me to enter the holy cloister,
the *giparu*,
and I went inside, I the high priestess Enheduanna!
I carried the ritual basket and sang your praise.
Now I am banished among the lepers.
Even I cannot live with you.
Shadows approach the light of day, the light
is darkened around me,

shadows approach the daylight,
covering the day with sandstorm.
My soft mouth of honey is suddenly confused.
My beautiful face is dust.

Restoration of Enheduanna to Her Former Station

The first lady of the throne room
has accepted Enheduanna's song.
Inanna loves her again.
The day is good for Enheduanna,
for she is dressed in her jewels.
She is dressed in her womanly beauty.
Like the moon's first rays over the horizon,
in her robes she is luxurious!
When Nanna, Inanna's father,
makes his entrance
the palace blesses Inanna's mother, Ningal.
From the doorsill of heaven comes the word:

"Welcome!"

(translated by Aliki Barnstone and Willis Barnstone)

QUEEN HATSHEPSUT
(D. 1482 BCE)

Pharaoh Queen Hatshepsut's Apologia

I sat in my palace, thinking of my maker,
And my heart said,
Make him two obelisks of electrum
Whose tops will touch heaven.
I erected them
In the holy Hall of Columns
Between two massive portals of the King,
The Strong Bull, King Aakheperkare, victorious Horus.

My heart wavers.
What will people say?
In later years surely they will see my monument
And talk about me.
Be sure to laugh at them when they utter,
"I don't know. I don't know.
Why was it built?
How was this gold mountain built
As if out of the blue?"

Hear my true words.
As I am loved by Re,
As my father Amun the Sungod favors me,
As life and dominion refresh my nostrils,
As I come out wearing the white crown,
As I come out wearing the red crown,
As the Two Lords joined their powers for me alone,
As I rule this land like the son of Isis,
As I am mighty like the son of Nut,
As Re lies down relaxing in his evening boat
As he prevails in his morning boat,
As he joins his two mothers in the ship of our gods,

As the sky prevails
And his creation is eternal,
As I shall be eternal like a deathless star,
As I shall lie down relaxing in life like Atum.

Hear my true words.
Through my majesty I erected these two giant obelisks of electrum
For my father Amun
So my name will prevail in this Karnak temple,
Forever and forever.
Each block is solid granite,
Seamless,
Without joining the other.

(translated by Aliki Barnstone and Willis Barnstone)

ANONYMOUS EGYPTIAN

(CA. 1500 BCE)

I find my love fishing

I find my love fishing
His feet in the shallows.

We have breakfast together
And drink beer.

I offer the magic of my thighs
He is caught in the spell.

(*translated by Ezra Pound and Noel Stock*)

ANONYMOUS JEW

(10TH–3RD CENTURIES BCE)

from the **Song of Songs**

I am black yet beautiful,
daughters of Jerusalem,
as black as Kedar's tents,
as lovely as Solomon's tapestries.
Don't look at me with scorn
because I am black,
because the sun has scorched me.

My mother's sons hated me.
They made me guardian of the vineyards
yet I failed to guard my own vineyard.
You whom my soul loves, tell me
where you graze your sheep,
where they lie down at noon.

Why should I wander veiled
among the flocks of your companions?

While the king lay on his couch
the spikenard aroma of my body filled the air.
My love is a sachet of myrrh
as he lies at night between my breasts.
My love is a cluster of henna blossoms
in the desert orchard of Ein Gedi.

An apple tree among young men.
I delight in his shadow

and lie before him
and his fruit is sweet to my tongue.

He led me to his drinking room
and his banner over me was love.

Feed me your raisins,
comfort me with apples,

for I am sick with love.
His left hand is under my head,

his right hand caresses my body.
O daughters of Jerusalem,

swear by the gazelles
and the deer of the hills

not to awake us
till after we have merged in love.

My lover is mine
and I am his.

He feeds his sheep
among the lilies.

Till day cools
and shadows tumble,

come stay with me.
Be a gazelle

or a young stag bounding
on jagged mountains.

Awake north wind and come south wind!
Blow on my garden, let the spices

be tossed about. Let my love come into
his garden and eat his precious fruits.

I am sleeping but my heart is awake.
My lover's voice is knocking:
"Open, let me in, my sister and darling, my dove and perfect one.
My head is soaked with dew,
my hair is wet with drops of night."

I have taken off my garments.
How can I put them on?
I have washed my feet.
How can I dirty them now?
My lover's hand shows at the door
and in me I burn for him.
I rise to open to my love,
my hands drip with liquid myrrh,
my fingers drench perfume
over the handle of the bolt.
I open to my love
but my love has turned and gone.
He has vanished.

When he spoke my soul vanished.
I look for him and can't find him.
I call. He doesn't answer.
The watchmen who go about the city
find me.
They beat me, they wound me,
they strip me of my mantle,
those guardians of the walls!

I beg you, daughters of Jerusalem,
if you find my love
you will say
that I am sick with love.

I go down to the orchard of nut trees
to see the green plants of the valley,
to see if the vines are in bud,
whether the pomegranates have blossomed.
Unaware, my soul leads me
into a chariot beside my prince.

I am my lover's
and he desires me.

Come, my love,
let us go out into the fields
and spend the night in villages.
Let us wake early and go to the vineyards
and see if the vine is in blossom,
if the new grape bud is open
and the pomegranates are in bloom.

There I will give you my love,
The mandrakes will spray aroma,
and over our door will be precious fruit,
all the new and old
that I have saved for you, my darling.

Oh, if you were my brother
who sucked my mother's breasts!

When I find you in the streets
or country, unshamed

I will kiss you
and no one will despise me.

I'll take you to my mother's home
and into her room

where she conceived me
and there you'll instruct me.

I'll give you spiced wine to drink,
the juice of my pomegranates.

Your left hand lies under my head,
your right hand caresses my body.

O daughters of Jerusalem,
I swear by the deer of the hills

not to wake us
till after we have merged in love.

I am a wall
and my breasts are towers,
and in his eyes
I bring peace.

(*translated by Willis Barnstone*)

SAPPHO
(B. 630–612 BCE)

Vision

Go so that
we can see
Lady Dawn
with gold arms,
which is
our fate.

World

I could not hope
to touch the sky
with my two arms.

Supreme Sight on the Black Earth

Some say cavalry and others claim
infantry or a fleet of long oars
is the supreme sight on the black earth.
I say it is

the one you love. And easily proved.
Didn't Helen, who far surpassed all
mortals in beauty, desert the best
of men, her king,

and sail off to Troy and forget
her daughter and her dear parents? Merely
Aphrodite's gaze made her readily bend
and led her far

from her path. These tales remind me now
of Anaktoria who isn't here,
yet I
for one

would rather see her warm supple step
and the sparkle of her face than watch all
the chariots in Lydia and foot soldiers armored
in glittering bronze.

Seizure

To me he seems like a god
the man who sits facing you
and hears you near as you speak
softly and laugh

in a sweet echo that jolts
the heart in my ribs. For now
as I look at you my voice
is empty and

can say nothing as my tongue
cracks and slender fire is quick
under my skin. My eyes are dead
to light, my ears

pound, and sweat pours over me.
I convulse, greener than grass,
and feel my mind slip as I
go close to death,

yet I must suffer all things,
being poor.

To Aphrodite (1)

On your dazzling throne, Aphrodite,
sly eternal daughter of Zeus,
I beg you: do not crush me
with grief

but come to me now—as once
you heard my far cry, and yielded,
slipping from your
father's house

to yoke the birds to your gold
chariot, and came. Handsome sparrows
brought you swiftly to
the dark earth,

their wings whipping the middle sky.
Happy, with deathless lips, you smiled:
"What is wrong, Sappho, why have
you called me?

What does your mad heart desire?
Whom shall I make love you,
who is turning her back
on you?

Let her run away, soon she'll chase you;
refuse your gifts, soon she'll give them.
She will love you, though
unwillingly."

Then come to me now and free me
from fearful agony. Labor
for my mad heart, and be
my ally.

Aphrodite of the Flowers at Knossos Coming Down from Heaven's Mountain

Leave Crete and come to this holy temple
where your graceful grove of apple trees
circles an altar smoking with frank-
    incense.

Here ice water babbles through the apple branches
and roses leave shadow on the ground
and bright shaking leaves pour down pro-
    found sleep.

In our meadow where the horses graze
amid wild blossoms of the spring and
anise shoots fill soft winds with a-
    roma

of honey, love goddess, pour heaven's
nectar carefully into gold wineglasses
and mingle our celebration with sud-
    den joy.

Return, Gongyla

Your lovely face.
When absent,
the pain of unpleasant
winter.

O Gongyla, my darling rose,
put on your milk-white gown. I want
you to come back quickly. For my
desire feeds on

your beauty. Each time I see your gown
I am made weak and happy. I too
blamed the Cyprus-born. Now I pray
she will not seek

revenge, and may she soon allow
you, Gongyla, to come to me
again: you whom of all women
I most desire.

To Aphrodite (2)

All the while
I prayed
our night would last
twice as long.

Dancers

The moon appeared in all her fullness
as virgins took their place around an altar.

In old days Cretan women danced
in perfect rhythm around a love alter,
crushing the soft flowering grass.

Evening Star

Hesperos, you bring home all the bright dawn
    scattered,
bring home the sheep,
bring home the goat, bring the child home to
    her mother.

Notice

The gods come
straightaway
to the tearless.

Age and Light

Here is success for your tongue, my children,
the poems of the pear-breasted Muses,

which are the fine gifts for the singer
on the clear tortoise lyre,

yet old age already wrinkles my skin,
my black hair has faded to white,

my legs can no longer carry me,
once nimble like a dancing fawn's,

but what can I do?
To be ageless is impossible,

no more than can the pink-armed Dawn
not end in darkness on the earth.

or keep her love for old Tithonos
who must waste away.

Yet I love refinement, and beauty and light
are for me the same as desire for the sun.

An Epiphany about Gongyla, Hermes and Hades

Gongyla, is there no sign of you? No epiphany
of your presence? Hermes came
in a dream. O Lord,

I swear by my ally Aphrodite, I have no pleasure
in being on the earth. I care
only to die,

to watch the banks of Acheron plaited
with lotus, the dewy banks
of the river of Hades.

Old Age

Of course I am downcast and tremble
with pity for my state
when old age and wrinkles cover me,

when Eros flies about
and I pursue the glorious young.
Pick up your lyre

and sing to us of her who wears
violets on her breasts. Sing especially
of her who is wandering.

Eros

Now in my
heart I
see clearly

a beautiful
face
shining,

etched
by love.

(*translated by Willis Barnstone*)

ZI YE (TZU YEH)
(6TH–3RD CENTURIES BCE?)

I heard my love was going to Yang-chou

I heard my love was going to Yang-chou
And went with him as far as Ch'u-shan.
For a moment when you held me fast in your outstretched arms
I thought the river stood still and did not flow.

All night I could not sleep

All night I could not sleep
because of the moonlight on my bed.
I kept on hearing a voice calling:
Out of Nowhere, Nothing answered "yes."

(*translated by Arthur Waley*)

PATACARA

(6TH–5TH CENTURIES BCE?)

Patacara Speaks

Young brahmins plough fields,
sow seeds,
nourish their wives and children,
get wealthy
Why can't I find peace?
I'm virtuous
comply with the teacher
not lazy or puffed up

One day washing my feet
I watched the water as it
trickled down the slope
I fixed my mind
the way you'd
train a thoroughbred horse

Later, taking my lamp
I enter my cell
sit on my bed and
watch the flame
I extinguish the wick
with a needle
The release of my mind
is like the quenching of the lamp
O the nirvana of the little lamp!

(*translated by Andrew Schelling and Anne Waldman*)

SANGHA
(6TH–5TH CENTURIES BCE?)

I gave up my house

I gave up my house
and set out into homelessness.
I gave up my child, my cattle,
and all that I loved.
I gave up desire and hate.
My ignorance was thrown out.
I pulled out craving
along with its root.
Now I am quenched and still.

(translated by Susan Murcott)

SAKULA

(6TH–5TH CENTURIES BCE?)

When I lived in a house

When I lived in a house
I heard a monk's words
and saw in those words
nirvana
the unchanging state.

I am the one
who left son and daughter,
money and grain,
cut off my hair
and set out into homelessness.

Under training
on the straight way,
desire and hatred fell away,
along with the obsessions
of the mind
that combine with them.

After my ordination,
I remembered
I had been born before.
The eye of heaven became clear.

The elements of body and mind
I saw as other,
born from a cause,
subject to decay.
I have given up the obsessions
of the mind.
I am quenched and cool.

(translated by Susan Murcott)

DANTIKA

(6TH–5TH CENTURIES BCE?)

As I left my daytime resting place

As I left my daytime resting place
on Vulture Peak,
I saw an elephant
come upon the riverbank
after its bath.

A man took a hook
and said to the elephant,
"Give me your foot."
The elephant stretched out its foot:
the man mounted.

Seeing what was wild before
gone tame under human hands,
I went into the forest
and concentrated my mind.

(*translated by Susan Murcott*)

NANDUTTA
(6TH–3RD CENTURIES BCE?)

Nanduttara

I used to worship
fire, the moon, sun,
all the gods
I used to go down
to the riverbanks
for the bathing rites
I took holy vows
shaved half my head
slept on the ground
wouldn't eat food after sundown
Then I decked myself
out with many ornaments
baths, unguents, massage—
you name it—
Tried everything
to stave off death
I was a slave to my body
Then I really "got" it
saw my body as it really is
went homeless
Lust? Sex?
Forget it
All that binds me head and foot
is loosened

(*translated by Andrew Schelling and Anne Waldman*)

ANONYMOUS BUDDHIST SISTER

(6TH–3RD CENTURIES BCE?)

An Anonymous Sister Speaks

It's been twenty-five years since I became a nun
But I'm still restless
No peace of mind—not even one moment
(*she snaps her fingers*)
Every thought's of sex
I hold out my arms
Cry out like a madwoman
Then I go into my cell
But I heard Dhamma-Dinna preach
and she taught me impermanence
I sat down to meditate:
I know I've lived before
My celestial eye has been purified
I see I see other lives past and present
I read other minds present and past
The ear element is purified
I hear I hear I can really hear

(*translated by Andrew Schelling and Anne Waldman*)

SISUPACALA
(6TH–3RD CENTURIES BCE?)

Sisupacala Speaks with Mara

Mara interrupts:
Don't forget where you've been before,
those other lives
you led in bittersweet realm
—animals, demons,
pretas your friends, companions—
Think about it, long for it
(*he whispers in her ear*)
Yearn again for the Kamaloka and the
seductive beauty of the dark
gods who rule in shadow
and the blissed-out gods
who rule by day
They'll take you, caress
your naked body . . .

She:
Stop, Mara
Don't you know those gods
go from birth to death to birth to
death again again,
become this, become that,
become this again, become that
You know the Kamaloka
stinks with lust
I tell you the world is blazing, blazing
the whole world's in flames
I tell you it's flared up
the world is shaken
your words are shaken
the whole world's ablaze!

(*translated by Andrew Schelling and Anne Waldman*)

SUMANGALA'S MOTHER
(6TH–3RD CENTURIES BCE?)

I am a free woman

I am a free woman,
at last free of slavery in the kitchen
where I walked back and forth
stained and squalid
among smelly cooking pots.
I got rid of
my brutal husband who ranked me lower
than the shade he sat in.
Purged of anger and the body's hunger
I meditate
in my own shade from a broad tree.

Here I am
serene.

(*translated by Willis Barnstone*)

GOVINDASVAMIN

(5TH CENTURY BCE–1000 CE?)

Holy sixth day

Holy sixth day
in the woods they worship the
trees then
then my heart beat hard
at how far I was going into
the woods
a snake appeared in front of me
and I fell down
I started writhing and rolling
this way and that way
my dress fell off
my hair burned along
my back
thorns scratched me
everywhere
suddenly who am I
who was I
how I
love those celebrations

(translated by W. S. Merwin and Moussaieff Masson)

ANONYMOUS SANSKRIT SONGS

(5TH CENTURY BCE–1000 CE?)

When he comes back

When he comes back
    to my arms

        I'll make him feel
        what nobody ever felt

        everywhere
        me
        vanishing into him

        like water
        into the clay of a new jar

My husband

My husband
before leaving on a journey
is still in the house speaking
to the gods and already
separation is climbing like
bad monkeys to the window

He who stole my virginity

He who stole my virginity
is the same man
I am married to
and these are the same
spring nights and
this is the same moment of

the jasmine's opening
with winds just coming of age carrying
the scent of its flowers mingled
with pollen from Kadamba trees
to wake desire
in its nakedness
I am no different yet I
long with my heart
for the delicate
love-making back there under
the dense cane-trees
by the bank of the river
Namanda in
the Vindhya mountains

(*translated by W. S. Merwin and Moussaieff Masson*)

PRAXILLA
(CA. 450 BCE)

Light and Earth

Most beautiful of things I leave is sunlight.
Then come glazing stars and the moon's face.
Then ripe cucumbers and apples and pears.

(*translated by Willis Barnstone*)

KORINNA

(LATE 3RD CENTURY BCE)

Hermes

When he sailed into the harbor
his ship became a snorting horse.

Hermes ravished the white city

while the wind like a nightingale
sang with its whirling war axe.

(*translated by Willis Barnstone*)

MIRYAM, MOTHER OF YESHUA (MARY, MOTHER OF JESUS)

(1ST CENTURY CE)

Song of Miryam
(The Magnificat)

My soul magnifies the Lord
and my spirit is joyful in God my savior,

for he looked upon his young slave
in her low station.

Hereafter all generations will call me blessed,
for through his powers the great one did wondrous

things for me. His name is holy.
His mercy goes from generation to generation

to those who fear him.
He has shown the strength of his arm

and scattered those who were proud
in the mind of their heart.

He has toppled monarchs from their thrones
and raised the poor to their feet.

He filled the hungry with good foods
and sent the rich away empty.

He has helped Israel his servant and child
through the memory of his mercy,

just as he spoke to our fathers,
to Avraham and to his everlasting seed.

(*translated by Willis Barnstone*)

ANONYMOUS INDIAN

(1ST CENTURY CE)

from the Gatha Saptashati

Clearly a god is kissing that lady,
making her nipples go stiff.
There is no way to approve of such a lover,
even if he is a god.

Let the love of harlots be sanctified.
After all, like the dalliance
of true love, it relieves
both the deep thirst and the hunger.

The gods have parceled him out,
his beauty caught in my eye,
his talk in my ears, heart in my
heart, his thing in my thing.

I remember this pleasure—
he sat at my feet
without speaking
and my big toe toyed with his hair.

Which would you have, sweetness
of sugar cane or that man's honeyed words?

Both cause bliss in the mind, blushes and goosebumps,
and make a girl want to be loved.

All who noticed expressed wonder.
She seemed no more than a girl.
But the touch of that first lover
gave her the breasts of a goddess.

A girl longing for dalliance
should never set out in the dark.
The flame of desire burns bright,
far too bright in the dark.

After our lovemaking
he takes one step away to look at the moon
and returns in five minutes,
but I feel bitterly abandoned.

O heart, you will be burnt
by one who has burnt many—a fire of a man,
and die in a flood
by one who drowns many—a flood of a man.

Only the lady who learns
how to make love to herself
knows how to deal with that anger
that leaves her half full, half empty.

With her eyes closed
she brought him to bed in her mind,
then did all the work with her hands
till her jingling bangles fell slack.

In the wayside inn the maid lay awake,
not happy until
she could hear the bangles of her mistress
jingling as that lady thrashed on her bed.

When her friends asked her why
saffron blossoms stuck to her breast
she brushed them away, only to reveal
bite marks of her lover, left and right.

He can no more see my sorrow
than a mirror sees in the dark.
Therefore I stumble in shadows
in a room he's abandoned forever.

I dance as he plays on his flute.
A creeper wraps wavering vines
round a tree with deep roots.
My love will never be steady like that.

If you can't bring him to his knees
with that glance like an arrow
and that musical walk you've perfected
he's a *sanyasi*, a holy man for sure.

Girl, no need to weep.
If you place the mango blossom
over your bosom and smile
he will be unable to pass you again.

These women plunder my husband
as if he were plums
in the bowl of a blind man.
But I can see them, clear as a cobra.

You love her while I love you,
and yet she hates you and says so.
Love ties us in knots,
keeps us in hell.

Friendship with a bad man—
a line drawn on water;
with a good man—etched forever,
deep script in white marble.

Good men can never be lovers,
for they must keep themselves constant,
tell the truth most of the time,
keep the tigers of passion in cages.

I don't know how we escaped.
We were tied in the strongest of nets,

and his arms made a tight cage around me.
Yet somehow, even my two breasts are free now.

Lakshmi, a goddess, was born from the sea.
Gods saw her glistening with foam.
And the travelers all halt, stare unblinking
at the plowman's daughter, wet from the river.

Let those who want sainthood
keep to their path of denial—no harm.
But I know what I want, and wait
for a chance for my eyes to say so.

The love gods have special affection
for women who like it on top,
their hair fanned out, disheveled,
eyes closed, their thighs trembling.

O heart, give me rest,
I've served love all too well,
but now, near the end,
let me feel no attachment.

She gathers Madhuka blossoms
weeping as if they were bones
of her husband, whom she had meant
to join on his funeral fire.

She was ready to follow,
into the fire of cremation, in suttee.
But because of her readiness, her hot love,
he came back to his life, joined her anew.

Even a god, when he mutters a mantra,
stumbles if he sees reflected
such a lotus-like face. Salute him,
but shun his bad habits. Pray with eyes closed.

(*translated by David Ray*)

ANONYMOUS GNOSTIC REVEALER

(2ND–3RD CENTURIES CE)

The Thunder and the Perfect Mind

I was sent out from the power
   and have come to you who study me
   and am found by you who seek me.
Look at me, you who study me,
   and you who hear, hear me.
You waiting for me, take me into yourselves.
Don't banish me from your vision.
Don't let hatred enter your voice against me, or let
   anger enter your hearing.
In no place, in no time, be unknowing of me. Be alert.
Don't be unknowing of me.

I am the first and the last.
I am the honored and scorned.
I am the whore and holy.
I am the wife and the virgin.
I am the mother and daughter.
I am the members of the family
and the barren one with many sons.
I have had a grand wedding
   and have not found a husband.
I am a midwife and do not give birth.
I am the solace of my labor pains.
I am bride and groom
   and my husband begot me.
I am the mother of my father
   and sister of my husband
   and he is my offspring.
I am a slave of him who prepared me
and ruler of my offspring.
He begot me earlier yet on a birthday.

He is my offspring to come
  and from him is my power.
I am the staff of his power in his youth
  and he the rod of my old age
  and whatever he wants happens to me.
I am a silence incomprehensible
  and an idea remembered often.
I am the voice whose sound is manifold
  and word whose appearance is multiple.
I am the utterance of my name.

(*translated by George W. McRae*)

AL-KHANSA
(575–646 CE)

Sleepless

I was sleepless, I was awake all night
as if my eyes exuded pus.

I watched the stars, though I was not their shepherd,
and veiled my body in ragged cloth,

for I heard—it was black news—
the messenger's report:

"Sakhr is in the earth,
between wood and stones."

Go, may Allah receive you, as a man
of justice and revenge.

Your heart was free,
its roots were not weak.

Like a spearhead your shape shines in the night,
strong, firm, the son of free men.

I lament our tribe's hero. Death took you
and the others.

As long as the ringdove cries, I'll mourn you,
as stars light the midnight traveler.

I'll not make peace with the enemy
till their food kettles turn white . . .

They washed the shame from you,
your blood's sweat poured out purified,

and war rode a humpbacked herd,
bareback.

Defender in battle,
you ripped the spearmen, tooth and nail,

until thousands saw you
blind to fear. They were amazed

as your stomach burst, punctured above the nipples,
spurting the foam of your heart's blood.

(*translated by Willis Barnstone*)

RABIA THE MYSTIC
(712–801)

You are the companion of my heart

You are the companion of my heart
Though my body I offer to those who desire it.

My body is friendly to guests

But you the companion of my heart
Are the guest of my soul.

Your prayers were light

Your prayers were light, your worship
was rest,
Your sleep an enemy of prayer.
The days of your life a chance
At which you failed.
Days pass and vanish slowly
And perish.

O my Lord, if I worship you

O my Lord, if I worship you
from fear of Hell,
Burn me in Hell.
If I worship you in hope of Paradise,
Exclude me.
If I worship you for you alone,
Do not withhold your eternal beauty.

O my Lord

O my Lord,
Stars glitter and human eyes are closed,
Kings lock their doors
And every lover is alone with love.
Here, I am alone with you.

(translated by Aliki Barnstone and Willis Barnstone)

YESHE TSOGYEL
(757?–817?)

This Supreme Being is the Dakini Queen of the Lake of Awareness!
I have vanished into fields of lotus-light, the plenum of dynamic space,
To be born in the inner sanctum of an immaculate lotus;
Do not despair, have faith!
When you have withdrawn attachment to this rocky defile,
This barbaric Tibet, full of war and strife,
Abandon unnecessary activity and rely on solitude.
Practise energy control, purify your psychic nerves and seed-essence,
And cultivate *mahamudra* and Dzokchen,

This Supreme Being is the Dakini Queen of the Lake of Awareness!
Attaining humility, through Guru Pema Jungne's compassion I followed
    him,
And now I have finally gone into his presence;
Do not despair, but pray!
When you see your karmic body as vulnerable as a bubble,
Realising the truth of impermanence, and that in death you are
    helpless,
Disabuse yourself of fantasies of eternity,
Make your life a practice of *sadhana,*
And cultivate the experience that takes you to the place where Ati ends.

(*translated by Keith Dowman*)

EDITOR'S NOTE: *Dakini* refers to the Buddhist notion of the inspiring power
of consciousness, often symbolized in Tibetan Buddhist iconography as a wrath-
ful naked female figure. *Mahamudra* ("the great seal") is the realization of emp-
tiness and the freedom from suffering. *Dzokchen* ("great perfection") refers to
the teaching that purity or perfection of mind is always present and need only be
recognized. *Sadhana* ("the means to perfection") is a type of meditation practice
involving detailed visualizations. *Ati,* or *ati-yoga* ("extraordinary yoga"), is an-
other term for *dzokchen.*

KASSIA

(CA. 840)

Mary Magdalene

Lord, this woman who fell into many sins
   perceives the God in you,
   joins the women bringing you myrrh,
   crying she brings myrrh   before your tomb.
"O what a night   what a night I've had!
   Extravagant frenzy   in a moonless gloom,
   craving the body.
Accept this spring of tears,
   you who empty seawater   from the clouds.
Bend to the pain   in my heart, you
   who made the sky bend   to your secret incarnation
   which emptied the heavens.
I will kiss your feet, wash them,
   dry them with the hair of my head, those feet whose steps
Eve heard at dusk
   in Paradise   and hid in terror.
Savior of souls   who will trace the plethora
   of my sins or the knowable chasm of your judgments?
Do not overlook me, your slave,
   in your measureless mercy."

(*translated by Aliki Barnstone, Willis Barnstone, and Elene Kolb*)

WU CAILUAN (WU TS'AILUAN)

(9TH CENTURY)

My mind is like a jade jar of ice,
Never invaded by even half a mote of dust.
Though the jade jar be obscured without,
I pay no mind at all—
On the terrace of Immortals,
I climb straight to the highest level.

Let the ox and horse be called,
To both I can respond—
But how could I let a speck of dust
Into the city of mind?
Favor and disgrace are meaningless—
What's the use of contending?
Drifting clouds do not obstruct the shining moonlight.

My body lives in the city,
But my essence dwells in the mountains.
The affairs of a puppet play
Are not to be taken too seriously.
When the polar mountain fits into a mustard seed,
All the words in the universe may as well be erased.

(*translated by Thomas Cleary*)

YU XUANJI (YÜ HSÜAN-CHI)
(843–868)

At the End of Spring

Deep lane, poor families; I have few friends.
He stayed behind only in my dream.

Fragrant silk scents the breeze: whose party?
A song comes carried in the wind: from where?

Drums in the street wake me at dawn.
In the courtyard, magpies mourn a spoiled spring.

How do we get the life we want?
I am a loosed boat floating a thousand miles.

Regretful Thoughts

Fallen leaves are scattered by evening rain.

I sing and brush red strings alone.

Unmoved by heartless friends,
I go within, beyond the bitter sea.

Outside my gate rumble rich men's carts.
By my pillow Taoist books are rolled.

Now in simple cottons, no more a guest of clouds,
No more green water and blue hills.

For Hidden Mist Pavilion

Spring flowers and autumn moon enter poems.
Bright days and clear nights are fit for idle gods.

Raised in vain the pearl screen, never lowered.
Long ago, I moved my couch to face the mountain.

Answering Li Ying Who Showed Me
His Poems about Summer Fishing

Though we lived in the same lane,
A whole year we didn't meet,

Until his tender phrases touched this aging woman.
I broke a new cinnamon branch.

The Tao nature cheats ice and snow.
The enlightened heart laughs at summer silks.

Footsteps climb the River of Clouds
Lost beyond roads in a sea of mist.

(*translated by Geoffrey Waters*)

ISE SHIKIBU (LADY ISE)
(9TH–10TH CENTURIES)

On Seeing the Field Being Singed

My body is like
a field wasted by winter.
If only
I, like the field burnt-over,
awaited the return of Spring!

Near a Waterfall at Ryumon

Hidden immortal,
whose garment has no break nor seam,
if you have gone from us
what mountain princess is this
displaying to us her white robes?

(translated by Etsuko Terasaki with Irma Brandeis)

IZUMI SHIKIBU (LADY IZUMI)

(CA. 974–1034)

From darkness
I go onto the road
of darkness.
Moon, shine on me from far
over the mountain edge.

Someone else
looked at the sky
with the same rapture
when the moon
crossed the dawn.

When you broke from me
I thought I let the thread
of my life break,
yet now, for you,
I don't want to die.

Orange leaves are gone,
ripped away by cold night
and winter rain.
If only yesterday we'd gone
to see the mountains!

If you love me,
come. The road
I live on
is not forbidden
by impetuous gods.

On this winter night
my eyes were closed
with ice.
I wore out the darkness
until lazy dawn.

Here in this world
I won't live
one minute more,
where pain is rank
like black bamboo.

(translated by Willis Barnstone)

ANONYMOUS JAPANESE TANKA

(10TH CENTURY?)

With every note

With every note
of the mountain temple
sunset bell
how sad to hear
day turn dark

(*translated by Willis Barnstone*)

ANONYMOUS LATIN SONG

(CA. 1000)

Planctus (*Lament*)

Wind is thin,
sun warm,
the earth overflows
with good things.

Spring is purple
jewelry;
flowers on the ground,
green in the forest.

Quadrupeds shine
and wander. Birds
nest. On blossoming
branches they cry joy!

My eyes see, my ears
hear so much, and
I am thrilled.
Yet I swallow sighs.

Sitting here alone,
I turn pale. When strong
enough to lift my head,
I hear and see nothing.

Spring, hear me.
Despite green woods,
blossoms and seed,
my spirit rots.

(*translated by Willis Barnstone*)

LI QINGZHAO (LI CH'ING-CHAO)
(1084–CA. 1151)

On the Earth and in Heaven

Rattan bed, paper netting. I wake from morning
sleep.
I can't reach the end of saying: I've no happy thoughts.
Incense flickers on, off. The jade burner is cold,
a companion to my feelings,
which are water.

I play three times with the flute,
astonishing a plum's heart.
How I feel spring's ache!
Slender wind and thin rain, tapping tapping.
Down come a thousand lines of tears.

The pipe-playing jade man is gone.
Empty tower.
My chest is broken. On whom can I lean?
I break off a twig.
On the earth and in heaven,
there's no one to send it to.

Where Am I Going?

Sky links cloud waves, links dawn fog.
The star river is about to turn. A thousand sails
    dance.
As if in dream my soul returns to god's home,
hearing heaven's voice,
eagerly asking: Where am I going back to?

I say: The road is long, the day near dusk;
in writing poems startling words come invisibly.

Ninety thousand miles of wind, the huge *peng* bird
    takes off.
Wind, don't stop.
the frail boat is to reach the three holy mountains.

Warm rain and sunny wind

Warm rain and sunny wind start to break
    the chill.
Willows like eyes, plums like cheeks.
I already feel spring's heart throbbing.
Wine and poems.
Whom can I share them with?
Tears dissolve my makeup. My gold hairpin
    is heavy.

I try on a light spring robe threaded with gold
and lean against a hill of pillows.
The hill damages the gold phoenix pin.
Alone I hug dense pain with no good dreams.
Late at night, I am still playing
as I trim the wick.

(*translated by Willis Barnstone and Sun Chu-chin*)

To the Tune of "Silk Washing Brook"

I don't need deep cups of thick amber wine.
My feelings will warm before I drown in drink.
Already sparse bells are answering the night wind.

Lucky Dragon incense fades as my soul-dream breaks.
From my loose hair drops a soft gold hairpin;
I wake alone and watch the red candle die.

To the Tune of "Dream Song"

I'll never forget sunset at Brook Pavilion—
drunk with beauty, we lost our way.
When the ecstasy faded, we turned out boat home,
but it was late and we strayed into a place deep
    with lotus flowers
and rowed hard, so hard
the whole shore erupted with herons and gulls.

To the Tune of "Spring at Wu Ling"*

The wind fades. Dropped blossoms perfume the earth.
At the end of the day, I'm too lazy to comb my hair.
His things remain, but he is gone, and the world is dead.
I try to speak but choke in tears.

I hear that spring is lovely at Twin Brook.
I'd row there in a light craft
but fear my grasshopper boat
is too small to carry this grief.

(*translated by Tony Barnstone and Chou Ping*)

Gates of Heaven

Year after year I have watched
My jade mirror. Now my rouge
And creams sicken me. One more
Year that he has not come back.
My flesh shakes when a letter
Comes from South of the River.
I cannot drink wine since he left.

———————
*Written after her husband's death.

But the Autumn has drunk up all my tears.
I have lost my mind, far off
In the jungle mists of the South.
The gates of Heaven are nearer
Than the body of my beloved.

(*translated by Kenneth Rexroth*)

HILDEGARD OF BINGEN
(1098–1179)

O how great is the miracle

O how great is the miracle
when the King entered
the submissive form of a woman!

God entered,
his humility rising over everything.

And how great is the joy filling her form!
The malice flowing from woman,
woman has erased.

She raised
the most delicate scent of virtue
and adorned the heavens
as once
she darkened the earth.

O Virgin in your diadem

O Virgin in your diadem of regal purple,
safe in the cloister
of your breastplate,

You bloomed fresh in the foliage
in other ways
than Adam who generated the human race.

Good morning! From your womb came fresh life
a life Adam stripped naked
from his children.

O flower, you didn't germinate in dew
or in drops of rain,
nor did wind soar over you,

but God's clear light made you spring noble
from a branch.

O branch, on the first day of his creation
God foresaw
your flowering.

And made you, O praised Virgin, into
gold matter for his Word.

O what great strength lies in a man's rib
out of which God shaped a woman.
He made you a mirror of all his beauty,
encompassing all his creations.

So the celestial organ chimes
and the whole earth
marvels, O praised Mary,
For God has loved you deeply.

O how darkly and profoundly we weep
for the sad crime
which flowed from the cunning serpent
into a woman.

Now, that woman
whom God made to be the mother of all
tore her womb with wounds
of ignorance
and gave birth to the heavy sorrow
of her children.

O dawn, in her womb he made
a new sun,
burning away all the crimes of Eve,
bringing blessings
greater
than Eve's harm to the race.

O Lady Savior,
you bore a new light
for us,
and gathered together
the followers of your Son
in celestial harmony.

Antiphon of the Gem Who Is Mary

O dazzling gem and serene glow of the sun,
a fountain from the Father's heart
has splashed into you,
his unique Word,
and with it he created the primordial stuff of the world,
and which Eve cast into confusion.
For you, Mary, the Father made a man with the Word.
You are the luminous earth
through whom the Word breathed forth
all the virtues of life,
just as from the primordial stuff
God released all creatures into life.

Virginal Lily

O how precious is the virginity
of the Virgin
whose door is closed
and whose womb
the Holy One flooded with his warmth
until a flower sprang in her,
and from her secret chamber
the Son of God
came like dawn.

Then her tender shoot,
who is her Son,

through the cloister of her womb
opened Paradise
and the Son of God
came like dawn.

(*translated by Aliki Barnstone and Willis Barnstone*)

SUN BUER (SUN PU-ERH)
(1124–?)

Nurturing the Child

The infant begins guileless,
One with light.
Then falls into the body, into time.

As soon as it breathes, a cry
Flies from its mouth,
And it is ruled by the tongue.

Not only that, it is burned out
By the sensual;
Indulgence traps it in sickness.

When the mother of the first light
Nurtures the child of time,
There is no need to talk more

Of turning back to the source.

(translated by Aliki Barnstone)

For Brightness, Eat Raw

If you eat live *chi,* raw energy,
Your lungs will be amazingly clear and cool.

If you forget spirit,
Illusion won't chain you.

If you merge with the union of yin and yang,
You will be free of numb emptiness.

Eat wild taro roots for breakfast.

At night as you wander hungry,
Pick shiny wetland mushrooms.

If you eat the hazy food of fire and smoke,
Your body won't walk on Jewel Pond.

(translated by Aliki Barnstone and Willis Barnstone)

ANONYMOUS PROVENÇAL

(12TH CENTURY)

My Lady Carenza of the lovely body

My Lady Carenza of the lovely body,
please offer sisters your profound advice,
and since you know what's best, tell us precise-
ly what to do. You know. Your ways embody
all ways of woman. Please say: shall I wed
someone we know? Or stay a virgin? I've said
that would be good. But having kids. What for?
To me a marriage seems a painful bore.

Lady Carenza, I'd like to have a man,
but what a penance when you have a clan
of brats. Your tits hang halfway to the ground;
your belly is discomfited and round.

My lady Iselda and my Lady Alais,
you have youth, beauty; your skin a fresh color
and you know courtly manners; you have valor
beyond all other women in your place.
Hear me. And for the best seed from a cod,
marry the Crown of Knowledge, who is GOD.
And you will bear the fruit in glorious sons,
saving your chastity like married nuns.

My Lady Iselda and my Lady Alais,
remember me and may my light erase
all fears. Please ask the king of glory, when
you enter heaven, to join us once again.

(translated by Willis Barnstone)

MAHADEVI

(12TH CENTURY)

Riding the blue sapphire mountains
wearing moonstone for slippers
blowing long horns
O Shiva
when shall I
crush you on my pitcher breasts?

O lord white as jasmine
when do I join you
stripped of body's shame
and heart's modesty?

People,
male and female,
blush when a cloth covering their shame
comes loose
        When the lord of lives
lives drowned without a face
in the world, how can you be modest?

When all the world is the eye of the lord,
onlooking everywhere, what can you
cover and conceal?

(*translated by A. K. Ramanujan*)

ZHU XUZHEN (CHU SHU-CHEN)

(CA. 1200)

Sorrow

The white moon gleams through scudding
Clouds in the cold sky of the Ninth
Month. The white frost weighs down the
Leaves and the branches bend low
Over the freezing water.
All alone I sit by my
Window. The crushing burden
Of the passing days never
Grows lighter for an instant.
I write poems, change and correct them,
And finally throw them away.
Gold chrysanthemums wither
Along the balcony. Hard
Cries of migrating storks fall
Heavily from the icy sky.
All alone by my window
Hidden in my empty room,
All alone, I burn incense,
And dream in the smoke, all alone.

(*translated by Kenneth Rexroth*)

ANONYMOUS FRENCH SONG

(12TH–13TH CENTURIES)

I am a young glad girl

I am a young glad girl, my way
graceful, not yet in my fifteenth year.
My breasts now sway
and swell.
I should be met
by love and hear
its lovely bell.
But I am in an awful prison!
God curse the villain,
the wicked sinner who put me
in a nunnery.
I can't stand religious life.
God, I'm too young!
In my belly I feel sweetly stung.
God curse the man who saddled me
as Jesus' wife.

(*translated by Aliki Barnstone and Willis Barnstone*)

BEATRICE OF NAZARETH

(CA. 1200–1268)

Grandeur of Love

Fish swim in the immensity of the oceans,
sleep near the bottom,

Birds dart above the highest wind
and boldly float in huge air,

So my soul freely wanders chasm, firmament,
and the grandeur of love.

(*translated by Aliki Barnstone and Willis Barnstone*)

MECHTHILD OF MAGDEBURG
(CA. 1212–1282)

How God Answers the Soul

It is my nature that makes me love you often,
For I am love itself.

It is my longing that makes me love you intensely,
For I yearn to be loved from the heart.

It is my eternity that makes me love you long,
For I have no end.

How the Soul Speaks to God

Lord, you are my lover,
My longing,
My flowing stream,
My sun,
And I am your reflection.

(*translated by Oliver Davies*)

MUKTABAI
(13TH CENTURY)

Where darkness is gone I live

Where darkness is gone I live,
where I am happy.
I am not troubled by coming and going,
I am beyond all vision,
above all spheres.
His spirit lives in my soul.

Mukta says: He is my heart's only home.

Though he has no form

Though he has no form
my eyes saw him,

his glory is fire in my mind
that knows

his secret inner form
invented by the soul.

What is
beyond the mind

has no boundary.
In it our senses end.

Mukta says: Words cannot hold him
yet in him all words are.

(*translated by Willis Barnstone*)

HADEWIJCH OF BRABANT

(13TH CENTURY)

Love Has Seven Names

Love has seven names.
Do you know what they are?
Rope, Light, Fire, Coal
make up its domain.

The others, also good,
more modest but alive:
Dew, Hell, the Living Water.
I name them here (for they
are in the Scriptures),
explaining every sign
for virtue and form.
I tell the truth in signs.
Love appears every day
for one who offers love.
That wisdom is enough.

Love is a ROPE, for it ties
and holds us in its yoke.
It can do all, nothing snaps it.
You who love must know.

The meaning of LIGHT
is known to those who
offer gifts to love,
approved or condemned.

The Scripture tell us
the symbol of COAL:
the one sublime gift
God gives the intimate soul.

Under the name of FIRE, luck,
bad luck, joy or no joy,
consumes. We are seized
by the same heat from both.

When everything is burnt
in its own violence, the DEW,
coming like a breeze, pauses
and brings the good.

LIVING WATER (its sixth name)
flows and ebbs
as my love grows
and disappears from sight.

HELL (I feel its torture)
damns, covering the world.
Nothing escapes. No one has grace
to see a way out.

Take care, you who wish
to deal with names
for love. Behind their sweetness
and wrath, nothing endures.
Nothing but wounds and kisses.

Though love appears far off,
you will move into its depth.

(*translated by Willis Barnstone and Elene Kolb*)

WANG QINGHUI
(WANG CH'ING-HUI)
(13TH CENTURY)

To the Tune of "The River Is Red"

Now the lotuses in the imperial lake
Must look entirely different from the old days.
I remember when I received the gracious
Rain and dew, in the Emperor's golden bed
In the jade palace, and my fame spread
Like orchid incense among the queens and concubines.
I blushed like a lotus blossom
Whenever I was summoned to my Lord's side.
Suddenly, one day, war drums on horseback
Came like thunder, tearing off the sky,
And all the glorious flowery days were gone forever.
Generals scattered like dragons and tigers.
Courtiers fled like clouds in the storm.
To whom can I tell
My everlasting sorrow for the dead?
I look out on the mountains and rivers of this fastness,
And my tears mingle with blood on my sleeves.
I wake in a posthouse from dreams of dust and dirt.
Fleeing in the dawn, our palace carts
Roll through the mountain pass
Under the setting moon.
I pray to Ch'ang-O,
The girl who fled for refuge to the moon,
And ask her to permit me
To follow her to safety.

(*translated by Kenneth Rexroth and Ling Chung*)

MARGUERITE PORETE
(D. 1310)

To the Reader of The Mirror of Simple Souls

To you the reader of this book,
Truly, if you care to understand,
Think what it says to you and look
Inside yourself. You must demand
Humility if you'd command
A way, for she's the treasurer
Of Science, and Virtue's mother.

Theologians and other clerks,
Give up. You do not have a clue.
However sharp your fine wit works,
If you don't choose to move into
Humility, Love and Faith who
Are the fair Ladies of the Mansion
Can't help you transcend mere Reason.

Humble your Science, bring it low,
For it is also based on Reason,
And gather everything you know
And bond it deep in any season
To what Love brings and Faith illumines.
Through love you'll know this book and give
What out of love makes the soul live.

The Soul and Christ the Chivalric Lover
from The Mirror of Simple Souls

She is alone in love, the phoenix alone.
The soul is solitary in love,
The soul has all and has nothing,

She knows all and knows nothing,
Yet she swims in the sea of joy,
Swims in the sea of delights flowing and streaming
Down from the godhead.
The soul feels no joy
For she is joy
Swimming and floating in joy.
She lives in joy. Joy lives in her.

Soul to Lover
from The Mirror of Simple Souls

Friend, what do you want of me?
I contain all that was, what is, and will be.
I hold all, standing tall.
Take everything from me you please.
I won't say no if you want all.
Say, friend, what do you want of me?
I am love. Love fills me end to end.
What you desire to fill
Your soul, we both desire, friend.
Say to us nakedly your will.

(*translated by Aliki Barnstone and Willis Barnstone*)

SAINT CATHERINE OF SIENA
(1347–1380)

Eternal Father, we were locked up in you

Eternal Father, we were locked up in you,
    in the garden under your ribs.
You drew us out of your holy mind
like a flower petaled with our soul's three powers,
and you placed the whole plant
    in each power
so the plant might bear fruit in your garden,
might go to you with the fruit
    you generated in her.
And you would come back to the soul
to fill her with bliss and holiness.
There the soul makes her home
    like the fish in the sea
    and the sea in the fish.

(*translated by Willis Barnstone*)

LAL DED (LALLA)
(14TH CENTURY?)

The soul, like the moon,
is new, and always new again.

And I have seen the ocean
continuously creating.

Since I scoured my mind
and my body, I too, Lalla,
am new, each moment new.

My teacher told me one thing,
Live in the soul.

When that was so,
I began to go naked,
and dance.

(*translated by Coleman Barks*)

I drag a boat over the ocean

I drag a boat over the ocean
with a solid rope.
Will God hear?
Will he take me all the way?
Like water in goblets of unbaked clay
I drip out slowly,
and dry.
My soul whirls. Dizzy. Let me
discover my home.

(*translated by Willis Barnstone*)

SISTER BERTKEN
(1427?–1514)

Garden

When I went into my garden, I found
only nettles and thorns.

The nettles and thorns I threw out.
I seeded some flowering plants.

I found someone who knew his work,
willing to help me in my task.

The tree was in such a hurry to climb,
I couldn't dig it out in time.

In my dilemma he had a remedy.
Alone he pulled up the tree.

Now I must ask advice from him
or he won't help me again.

However much I weed and clear,
the poison grass appears.

I'd like to seed lilies on this site
before the day is bright.

If my lover feeds it with dew,
it will richly bloom.

He loves among all flowers,
the lily in its white splendor.

Red roses unfurl.
In their calices burns the pearl.

Then the pearl is dressed in sun.
The strong heart looks on.

Jesus is the gardener's name.
I am his. One being, we are the same.

His love is sweetest breath,
beyond all things on earth.

(*translated by Willis Barnstone*)

ANONYMOUS NAHUATL
(15TH CENTURY)

Poem to Ease Birth

in the house with the tortoise chair
   she will give birth to the pearl
           to the beautiful feather

in the house of the goddess who sits on a tortoise
   she will give birth to the necklace of pearls
           to the beautiful feathers we are

there she sits on the tortoise
   swelling to give us birth

on your way on your way
   child be on your way to me here
       you whom I made new

come here child   come be pearl
         be beautiful feather

Poem to Be Recited Every Eight Years
While Eating Unleavened Tamales

[1]

the flower
   my heart
      it opened
at midnight
   that lordly hour

she has arrived
       Tlaçolteotl
         our mother
           goddess desire

[2]

in the birth house
in the flower place
on the day called 'one flower'
    the maize god is born

in the vapor and rain place
    where we go angling for jewel-fish

    where we too make our young

[3]

soon day   red sky
quechol-birds in the flowers

[4]

down here on earth
    you rise in the market place and say
I am the lord Quetzalcoatl

let there be gladness among the flowering trees
    and the quechol-bird tribes
who are the souls of the brave

may they rejoice
    hear the word of our lord
the quechol-bird's word

'your brother whom we mourn
    will never be killed again
never again will the poison dart strike him'

[5]

maize flowers
    white and yellow
I have brought from the flower place

see there is the lord of the jewel land
    playing ball in his holy field

there he is the old dog god
          Xolotl

[6]

now go look if Piltzintecutli
    lord fertility himself
has yet lain down in the dark house
        in the house where it grows dark

o Piltzintli Piltzintli
    yellow feathers
you glue all over yourself

on the ball-playing field you lie down
        and in the dark house where it grows dark

[7]

here comes a merchant

a vassal of Xochiquetzal
    mistress of Cholula

(heart o heart
    I fear the maize god is still on his way)

a merchant a man from Chacalla
    sells turquoise spikes for your ears
and turquoise bands for your arms

[8]

the sleeper the sleeper he sleeps

with my hand I have rolled him to sleep

[9]

here
        the woman
here
        am I
here
            asleep

(*translated by Anselm Hollo*)

84   ANONYMOUS NAHUATL

VITTORIA DA COLONNA
(1492–1547)

I live on this depraved and lonely cliff

I live on this depraved and lonely cliff
like a sad bird abhorring a green tree
or plashing water. I move forcefully
away from those I love, and I am stiff
even before myself so that my thoughts
may rise and fly to him: sun I adore
and worship. Though their wings could hurry more,
they race only to him. The forest rots
until the instant when they reach that place.
Then deep in ecstasy, though quick, they feel
a joy beyond all earthly joy. I reel,
and yet if they could recreate his face
as my mind craving and consuming would,
then here perhaps I'd own the prefect good.

(*translated by Willis Barnstone*)

HUANG E (HUANG O)
(1498–1569)

To the Tune of "Soaring Clouds"

You held my lotus blossom
In your lips and played with the
Pistil. We took one piece of
Magic rhinoceros horn
And could not sleep all night long.
All night the cock's gorgeous crest
Stood erect. All night the bee
Clung trembling to the flower
Stamens. Oh my sweet perfumed
Jewel! I will allow only
My Lord to possess my sacred
Lotus pond, and every night
You can make blossom in me
Flowers of fire.

(*translated by Kenneth Rexroth and Ling Chung*)

MIRABAI
(CA. 1498–1573)

He took his sword

He took his sword and cut me
open. I'm lame. My ears
are dead. I don't see.
No one knows why I sit here forever,
waiting.
He can repair me. If you don't believe me,
ask the ancient Vedas.
I mope outside the walls of paradise.

The night is painted red

The night is painted red
and I am ready,
dressed to get undressed.
This is my night
with the king.
The sheets are fresh.
My eyes have their dark coloring.
I am jasmine with its night aroma.
I'm so happy I go out
tossing gems to the hungry.
He has put on his beautiful
dark face.
I am happy
because now my wedding night
is eternity.
What hurt me is gone.
Don't worry, friend. I'm
lucky.
The Braj prince is mine

with his habit
of mountain holding and flute playing.
I don't have to go through
birth after birth.
He's taken me.

Mira is dancing

Mira is dancing with bells tied
on her ankles.
People say Mira has gone mad.

Her mother-in-law is upset
at the ruined family honor.

The king sends her a cup of poison.
Laughing, she drinks it
for her drink is Hari's beautiful face.

She has offered her body and her soul
at Hari's feet.
She drinks the honey of her vision.
Only he
is her ultimate protector.

Rama is my box of gems

Rama is my box of gems.
It's mine.
I can't trade it in the market.
A thief can't get at me.
It increases daily.
It can't sink, burn, and the earth
can't contain it.
His name is the boat and he, my Guru,
is the boatman.
I am with him, and he is rowing,
he is rowing me across.

When I don't see you

When I don't see you
I ache
uncontrollably.
For you
I give up everything
and become an ascetic.
I tramp every foot of the town,
gardens, forests.
I have decided on death by fire,
to be a *sati*.
If through fire I am mere ashes,
if I am ashes
on your body,
maybe we'll be one.
A sea of pleasure.

Here is my dress

Here is my dress. With him
my *sari* is forgiveness.
Rama's name is its gold hem.
The vermillion dot on my forehead is Rama.
His holy word is my nose diamond.
I wake to him in my braceleted arms.
He is also wrapped around my wrists
as glassy red bangles.
I put my clothes on after we leave the bed.

The charmer stole my ring

The charmer stole my ring.
Stop him. He carried it off
into the remote Himalayas.
We met in a grove
when I was selling curds.
I looked for him everywhere,

in Mathura, in Gokul.
I asked the fortune teller.
He said the thief is the dark prince.
He carried off my heart soul
and the ring.
I am wandering the earth,
looking for your face.
Where are you?

My love is in my house

My love is in my house,
I watched the road for years
but never saw him.
I put out the worship plate,
gave away gems.
After this, he sent word.
My dark lover has come,
joy is on my limbs.
Hari is an ocean,
my eyes touch him.
Mira is an ocean of joy.
She takes him inside.

No, it is not possible

No, it is not possible
to throw away this love.
I'm a leaf
with the sickness of late autumn.
Maybe it is jaundice.
I don't eat,
thinking penance may recreate
my lover.
Restless, I stand
at the door by the courtyard
or up in the palace turret.
I go about with a knife

in my shoulders.
No one sees it.
They call a doctor to look me over.
He is an idiot.
What does he know about cracked souls!

(*translated by Willis Barnstone and Usha Nilsson*)

ANONYMOUS SPANISH SONGS
(15TH–16TH CENTURIES)

Under the oak tree

Under the oak tree, oak tree,
under the oak tree.

I was on my way, mother,
to a pilgrimage.
To be more devout
I took no companion
under the oak tree.

To be more devout
I took no companion.
I took another road,
left the one I knew
under the oak tree.

Soon I was lost
on a small mountain,
and fell into sleep
at the foot of an oak
under the oak tree.

In the middle of night
I woke—what a plight!—
and was in the arms
of him I loved most
under the oak tree.

It hurt me, grieved me
that it was dawning.
I was enjoying
him I loved most
under the oak tree.

Very blessed be
every pilgrimage
under the oak tree.

Since I'm a girl

Since I'm a girl
I want fun.
It won't help God
for me to be a nun.
Since I'm a girl
with long hair,
they want to dump me
in a convent.
It won't help God
for me to be a nun.
Since I'm a girl,
I want fun.
It won't help God
for me to be a nun.

(*translated by Willis Barnstone*)

LOUISE LABÉ
(1525–1566)

White Venus

White Venus limpid wandering in the sky,
hear my voice. It sings to you. Its cares grow
while your high face makes the firmament glow.
It is weary, filled with worry. Now my eye
will be more tender, straining to stay awake,
and it will cry more tears and it will stare
at you. My pillow will be drenched. Your car-
ing eye is certain witness to my ache.
But people have a feeble spirit. They need
to lie down, fade away, and deeply feed
on sleep. I suffer now in the sun's light
and when I'm almost broken, pierced, and when
abandoned in my lonely bed, it's then
I must scream out my misery through the night.

Lute, companion of my calamity

Lute, companion of my calamity,
unblamable witness of my sighs, ver-
itable assessor of my gray despair,
often you have shared your lament with me.
So many tears have fallen constantly
on you, that when you are to sing a rare
and happy sound, you hide it unaware,
converting the white song to agony
And if I want to force you to rejoice,
you silence me by loosening a string.
But when my gentle sighs enter your being,
then you approve of my unhappy voice
and my hurt makes me cheerful like a friend
and from sweet pain I hope for a sweet end.

If I could linger on his lovely chest

If I could linger on his lovely chest
happy, soaring with him for whom I see
myself die, if envy did not keep me
from living my brief days with him, and best,
if holding me he'd say: "My dear friend,
let us enjoy each other and be sure
that no rainburst or seas or seastorm lure
us to separation before our lives end,"
if, while my arms were sleeping on the nape
of his neck like ivy circling a tree,
death came, jealous of our carefree rapport
as tenderly he kissed me more and more,
into his lips my soul would then escape
and, more than alive, I'd die in ecstasy.

(translated by Aliki Barnstone and Willis Barnstone)

EMILIA LANIER
(1569–1645)

Eves Apologie

Till now your indiscretion sets us free
And makes our former fault much less appeare;
Our Mothere *Eve,* who tasted of the Tree,
Giving to *Adam* what shee held most deare,
Was simply good, and had no powre to see,
The after-comming harme did not appeare:
 The subtile Serpent that our Sex betraide,
 Before our fall so sure a plot had laide.

That undiscerning Ignorance perceav'd
No guild, or craft that was by him intended;
For had she knowne, of what we were bereav'd,
To his request she had not condiscended.
But she (poor soule) by cunning was deceav'd,
No hurt therein her harmelesse Heart intended:
 For she alleadg'd Gods word, which he denies,
 That they should die, but even as Gods, be wise.

But surely *Adam* can not be excusde,
Her fault though great, yet hee was most too blame;
What Weaknesse offered, Strength might have refusde,
Being Lord of all, the greater was his shame:
Although the Serpents craft had her abusde,
Gods holy word ought all his actions frame,
 For he was Lord and King of all the earth.
 Before poore *Eve* had either life or breath.

Who being fram'd by Gods eternall hand,
The perfect'st man that ever breath'd on earth;
And from Gods mouth receiv'd that strait command,
The breach whereof he knew was present death:
Yea having powre to rule both Sea and Land,

Yet with one Apple wonne to loose that breath
    Which God had breathed in his beauteous face,
    Bringing us all in danger and disgrace.

And then to lay the fault on Patience backe,
That we (poore women) must endure it all;
We know right well he did discretion lacke,
Beeing not perswaded thereunto at all;
If *Eve* did erre, it was for knowledge sake,
The fruit being faire perswaded him to fall:
    No subtile Serpents falshood did betray him,
    If he would eate it, who had powre to stay him?

Not *Eve,* whose fault was onely too much love,
Which made her give this present to her Deare,
That what shee tasted, he likewise might prove,
Whereby his knowledge might become more cleare;
He never sought her weakenesse to reprove,
With those sharpe words, which he of God did heare:
    Yet Men will boast of Knowledge, which he tooke
    From *Eves* fair hand, as from a learned Booke.

If any Evill did in her remaine,
Beeing made of him, he was the ground of all;
If one of many Worlds could lay a staine
Upon our Sexe, and worke so great a fall
To wretched Man, by Satans subtile traine;
What will so fowle a fault amongst you all?
    Her weakenesse did the Serpents words obay,
    But you in malice Gods deare Sonne betray.

Whom, if unjustly you condemne to die,
Her sinne was small, to what you doe commit:
All mortal sinnes that doe for vengeance crie,
Are not to be compared unto it:
If many worlds would altogether trie,
By all their sinnes the wrath of God to get;
    This sinne of yours, surmounts them all as farre
    As doth the Sunne, another little starre.

Then let us have our Libertie againe,
And challendge to your selves no Sov'raigntie;

You came not in the world without our paine,
Make that a barre against your crueltie;
Your fault being greater, why should you disdaine
Our beeing your equals, free from tyranny?
    If one weake woman simply did offend,
    This sinne of yours, hath no excuse, nor end.

SOR VIOLANTE DO CÉU
(1602?–1693)

Voice of a Dissipated Woman Inside a Tomb
Talking to Another Woman Who Presumed to Enter a
Church with the Purpose of Being Seen and Praised by
Everyone, Who Sat Down Near a Sepulcher Containing
This Epitaph, Which Curiously Reads

You fool yourself and live a crazy day
or year, dizzy with adventures, and bent
solely on pleasures! Know the argument
of rigid doom and find a wiser way.
Consider that here, buried in the earth,
a dazzling and commended beauty lies,
and all live things are nothing, dust, and worth
less than the nothing of your life and lies.
Consider that when rigid death is come,
it laughs at beauty and discernment, and
what seems entirely certain fades in doubt.
Learn from this tomb what you will soon become,
and live more prudently till that command
is heard: the end which ends with no way out.

(*translated by Willis Barnstone*)

ANNE BRADSTREET
(1612?–1672)

Before the Birth of One of Her Children

All things within this fading world hath end,
Adversity doth still our joys attend;
No ties so strong, no friends so dear and sweet,
But with death's parting blow is sure to meet.
The sentence past is most irrevocable,
A common thing, yet oh, inevitable.
How soon, my Dear, death may my steps attend,
How soon't may be thy lot to lose thy friend,
We both are ignorant, yet love bids me
These farewell lines to recommend to thee,
That when that knot's untied that made us one,
I may seem thine, who in effect am none.
And if I see not half my days that's due,
What nature would, God grant to yours and you;
The many faults that well you know I have
Let be interred in my oblivious grave;
If any worth or virtue were in me,
Let that live freshly in thy memory
And when thou feel'st no grief, as I no harms,
Yet love thy dead, who long lay in thine arms.
And when thy loss shall be repaid with gains
Look to my little babes, my dear remains.
And if thou love thyself, or loved'st me,
These O protect from step-dame's injury.
And if chance to thine eyes shall bring this verse,
With some sad sighs honour my absent hearse;
And kiss this paper for thy love's dear sake,
Who with salt tears this last farewell did take.

Here Follows Some Verses
upon the Burning of Our House
July 10th, 1666.
Copied Out of a Loose Paper

In silent night when rest I took
For sorrow near I did not look
I wakened was with thund'ring noise
And piteous shrieks of dreadful voice.
That fearful sound of "Fire!" and "Fire!"
Let no man know is my desire.
I, starting up, the light did spy,
And to my God my heart did cry
To strengthen me in my distress
And not to leave me succorless.
Then, coming out, beheld a space
The flame consume my dwelling place.
And when I could no longer look,
I blest His name that gave and took,
That laid my goods now in the dust.
Yea, so it was, and so 'twas just.
It was His own, it was not mine,
Far be it that I should repine;
He might of all justly bereft
But yet sufficient for us left.
When by the ruins oft I past
My sorrowing eyes aside did cast,
And here and there the places spy
Where oft I sat and long did lie:
Here stood that trunk, and there that chest,
There lay that store I counted best.
My pleasant things in ashes lie,
And them behold no more shall I.
Under thy roof no guest shall sit,
Nor at thy table eat a bit.
No pleasant tale shall e'er be told,
Nor things recounted done of old.
No candle e'er shall shine in thee,
No bridegroom's voice e'er heard shall be.

In silence ever shall thou lie,
Adieu, Adieu, all's vanity.
Then straight I 'gin my heart to chide,
And did thy wealth on earth abide?
Didst fix thy hope on mold'ring dust?
The arm of flesh didst make thy trust?
Raise up thy thoughts above the sky
That dunghill mists away may fly.
Thou hast an house on high erect,
Framed by that mighty Architect,
With glory richly furnished,
Stands permanent though this be fled.
It's purchased and paid for too
By Him who hath enough to do.
A price so vast as is unknown
Yet by His gift is made thine own;
There's wealth enough, I need no more,
Farewell, my pelf, farewell my store.
The world no longer let me love,
My hope and treasure lies above.

In Memory of My Dear Grandchild Anne Bradstreet Who Deceased June 20, 1669, Being Three Years and Seven Months Old

With troubled heart and trembling hand I write,
The heavens have changed to sorrow my delight.
How oft with disappointment have I met,
When I on fading things my hopes have set?
Experience might 'fore this have made me wise,
To value things according to their price.
Was ever stable joy yet found below?
Or perfect bliss without mixture of woe?
I knew she was but as a withring flower,
That's here today, perhaps gone in an hour;
Like as a bubble, or the brittle glass,
Or like a shadow turning as it was.

More fool than I to look on that was lent
As if mine own, when thus impermanent.
Farewell dear child, thou ne're shall come to me,
But yet a while, and I shall go to thee;
Mean time my throbbing heart's cheered up with this:
Thou with my Saviour art in endless bliss.

SOR JUANA INÉS DE LA CRUZ
(1648/51–1695)

To Her Portrait

What you see here is colorful illusion,
an art boasting of beauty and its skill,
which in false reasoning of color will
pervert the mind in delicate delusion.
Here where the flatteries of paint engage
to vitiate the horrors of the years,
where softening the rust of time appears
to triumph over oblivion and age,
all is a vain, careful disguise of clothing,
it is a slender blossom in the gale,
it is a futile port for doom reserved,
it is a foolish labor that can only fail:
it is a wasting zeal and, well observed,
is corpse, is dust, is shadow, and is nothing.

(*translated by Willis Barnstone*)

In Which She Satisfies a Fear
with the Rhetoric of Tears

This afternoon, my love, speaking to you
since I could see that in your face and walk
I failed in coming close to you with talk,
I wanted you to see my heart. Love, who
supported me in what I longed to do,
conquered what is impossible to gain.
Amid my tears that were poured out in pain,
my heart became distilled and broken through.
Enough, my love. Don't be so stiff. Don't let

these maddening jealousies and arrogance
haunt you or let your quiet be upset
by foolish shadows: false signs of a man's
presence; and as you see my heart which met
your touch—now it is liquid in your hands.

(*translated by Aliki Barnstone and Willis Barnstone*)

To Hope

A green beguilement in our natural life,
mad hope and frenzy wrapped about with gold,
a dream by those awake, yet thinly cold
like dreams and treasures rife, with illusions.
Soul of the world, exuberant old age,
decrepit greenness of pure fantasy,
the now for which the happy ones rampage,
the future where the miserable would be.
Clutching your name, seeking your day as real,
they stick green lenses in their glasses, and
the world they see is painted by command.
But I, much saner in my state of mind,
keep both eyes focused on my hands. Not blind,
I only see what I can touch and feel.

(*translated by Willis Barnstone*)

from First Dream

But Venus first
with her fair gentle morning-star
shone through the dayspring,
and old Tithonus' beauteous spouse
—Amazon in radiance clad—
armed against the night,
fair though martial
and though plaintive brave,

showed her lovely brow
crowned with morning glimmers,
tender yet intrepid harbinger
of the fierce luminary
that came, mustering his van
of tiro gleams
and his rearward
of stouter veteran lights
against her, usurping tyrant
of day's empire, who,
girt with gloom's black bays
sways with dread nocturnal sceptre
the shades,
herself by them appalled.
But the fair forerunner,
herald of the bright sun,
scarce flew her banner in the orient sky,
calling all the sweet if warlike
clarions of the birds to arms,
their featly artless
sonorous bugles,
when the doomed tyrant, trembling,
distraught with dread misgiving,
striving the while
to launch her vaunted might, opposing
the shield of her funereal cloak
in vain to the unerring
shafts of light
with the rash unavailing
valiance of despair,
sensible of her faintness to withstand,
prone already to commit to flight,
more than to might, the means of her salvation,
wound her raucous horn,
summoning her black battalions
to orderly retreat.
Forthwith she was assailed
with nearer plentitude of rays
of the world's lofty towers.
The sun in truth, its circuit closed, drew near,

limning with gold on sapphire blue a thousand
times a thousand points and gleaming scarves,
and from its luminous circumference
innumerable rays of pure light streamed,
scoring the sky's cerulean plain,
and serried fell on her who was but now
the baneful tyrant of their empire.
She, flying in headlong rout,
mid her own horrors stumbling,
trampling on her shade,
strove, with her now blindly fleeing host
of shadows harried by the overtaking light,
to gain the western verge which loomed at last
before her impetuous course.
Then, by her very downfall vivified,
plunging in ever more precipitant ruin,
with renewed rebellion she resolves,
in that part of the globe
forsaken by the day,
to wear the crown,
what time upon our hemisphere the sun
the radiance of his fair golden tresses shed,
with equable diffusion of just light
apportioning to visible things their colours
and still restoring
to outward sense its full efficacy,
committing to surer light
the world illuminated and myself awake.

(*translated by Samuel Beckett*)

PHILLIS WHEATLEY
(1753–1784)

On Being Brought from Africa to America.

'Twas mercy brought me from my *Pagan* land,
Taught my benighted soul to understand
That there's a God, that there's a *Saviour* too:
Once I redemption neither sought nor knew.
Some view our sable race with scornful eye,
"Their colour is a diabolic die."
Remember, *Christians*, *Negros*, black as *Cain*,
May be refin'd, and join th' angelic train.

ANNETTE VON DROSTE-HÜLSHOFF
(1797–1848)

The Last Day of the Year (New Year's Eve)

The year at its turn,
the whirring thread unrolls.
One hour more, the last today,
and what was living time is scrolls
of dust dropping into a grave.
I wait in stern

silence. O deep night!
Is there an open eye?
Time, your flowing passage shakes
these walls. I shiver, my
one need is to observe. Night wakes
in solitude. I light

my eyes to all
that I have done and thought.
All that was in my head and heart
now stands like sullen rot
at Heaven's door. Victory in part—
the rest a fall

into dark wind
whipping my house! Yes, this year
will shatter and ride on the wings
of storm; not breathe under the clear
light of stars like quiet things.
You, child of sin,

has there not been
a hollow, secret quiver each
day in your savage chest,
as the polar winds reach

across the stones, breaking, possessed
with slow and in-

sistent rage? Now my lamp
is about to die; the wick
greedily sucks the last drop of oil.
Is my life like smoke lick-
ing the oil? Will death's cave uncoil
before me black, damp?

My life breaks down
somewhere in the circle of
this year. Long have I known
decay. Yet my heart in love
glows under the huge stone
of passion. I frown,

sweating in deep
fear, my hands, forehead wet.
Why? Is there a moist star
burning through clouds? Is it
the star of love, with far
light, dim from fear, a steep

booming note. Do you hear?
Again! Song for the dead!
The bell shakes in its mouth.
O Lord, on my knees I spread
my arms, and from my drouth
beg mercy. Dead is the year!

(*translated by Willis Barnstone*)

WU ZAO (WU TSAO)
(19TH CENTURY)

For the Courtesan Ch'ing Lin

On your slender body
Your jade and coral girdle ornaments chime
Like those of a celestial companion
Come from the Green Jade City of Heaven.
One smile from you when we meet,
And I become speechless and forget every word.
For too long you have gathered flowers,
And leaned against the bamboos,
Your green sleeves growing cold,
In your deserted valley:
I can visualize you all alone,
A girl harboring her cryptic thoughts.

You glow like a perfumed lamp
In the gathering shadows.
We play wine games
And recite each other's poems.
Then you sing, "Remembering South of the River"
With its heartbreaking verses. Then
We paint each other's beautiful eyebrows,
I want to possess you completely—
Your jade body
And your promised heart.
It is Spring.
Vast mists cover the Five Lakes.
My dear, let me buy a red painted boat
And carry you away.

(translated by Kenneth Rexroth and Ling Chung)

ELIZABETH BARRETT BROWNING
(1806–1861)

from Sonnets from the Portuguese

When our two souls stand up erect and strong,
Face to face, silent, drawing nigh and nigher,
Until the lengthening wings break into fire
At either curvèd point—what bitter wrong
Can the earth do to us, that we should not long
Be here contented? Think. In mounting higher,
The angels would press on us and aspire
To drop some golden orb of perfect song
Into our deep, dear silence. Let us stay
Rather on earth, Belovèd—where the unfit
Contrarious moods of men recoil away
And isolate pure spirits, and permit
A place to stand and love in for a day,
With darkness and the death-hour rounding it.

To George Sand, a Recognition

True genius, but true woman! dost deny
The woman's nature with a manly scorn
And break away the gauds and armlets worn
By weaker women in captivity?
Ah, vain denial! that revolted cry
Is sobbed in by a woman's voice forlorn—
Thy woman's hair, my sister, all unshorn,
Floats back dishevelled strength in agony,
Disproving thy man's name; and while before
The world thou burnest in a poet-fire
We see thy woman-heart beat evermore
Through the large flame. Beat, purer, heart, and higher,
Till God unsex thee on the heavenly shore
Where unincarnate spirits purely aspire!

BIBI HAYATI
(D. 1853)

Before there was a hint of civilization

Before there was a hint of civilization
I carried a memory of your loose strand of hair,
Oblivious, I carried inside me your pointed tip of hair.

In its invisible realm,
Your face of sun yearned for epiphany,
Until each distinct thing was thrown into sight.

From the first instant time took a breath,
Your love lay in the soul,
A treasure in the secret chest in the heart.

Before the first seed shot up out of the rose bed of the possible,
The soul's lark took wing high above your meadow,
Flying home to you.

I thank you one hundred times! In the altar
Of Hayati's eyes, your face shines
Forever present and beautiful.

Is it the night of power

Is it the night of power
Or only your hair?
Is it dawn
Or your face?

In the songbook of beauty
Is it a deathless first line
Or only a fragment
Copied from your inky eyebrow?

Is it boxwood of the orchard
Or cypress of the rose garden?
The tuba tree of paradise, abundant with dates,
Or your standing beautifully straight?

Is it musk of a Chinese deer
Or scent of delicate rosewater?
The rose breathing in the wind
Or your perfume?

Is it scorching lightning
Or light from fire on Sana'i Mountain?
My hot sigh
Or your inner radiance?

Is it Mongolian musk
Or pure ambergris?
Is it your hyacinth curls
Or your braids?

Is it a glass of red wine at dawn
Or white magic?
Your drunken narcissus eye
Or your spell?

Is it the Garden of Eden
Or heaven on earth?
A mosque of the masters of the heart
Or a back alley?

Everyone faces a mosque of adobe and mud
When they pray.
The mosque of Hayati's soul
Turns to your face.

How can I see the splendor of the moon

How can I see the splendor of the moon
If his face shines over my heart,
Flaming like the sun?

The Turks in his eyes charge through my soul,
While untrue curling hair
Defeats faith.

Yet if he lifted the veil from his face,
The world would be undone,
The universe astounded.

He walks through the garden
With grace, erect,
His exquisite posture mocking even the straight cypresses.

He charges, riding his gnostic horse
Into the holy space of divinity,
The sacred sphere.

Tonight the Saki with its red-stained ruby lips
Pours wine for the luxury of every drunk,
And sates every reveler's taste.

As Hayati has drunk his ecstasy,
Her soul now satisfied by the wine of his pure heart,
How can she drink any other nectar?

(translated by Aliki Barnstone)

CHARLOTTE BRONTË
(1816–1855)

Speak of the North

Speak of the North! A lonely moor
Silent and dark and trackless swells,
The waves of some wild streamlet pour
Hurriedly through its ferny dells.

Profoundly still the twilight air,
Lifeless the landscape; so we deem
Till like a phantom gliding near
A stag bends down to drink the stream.

And far away a mountain zone,
A cold, white waste of snow-drifts lies,
And one star, large and soft and lone,
Silently lights the unclouded skies.

EMILY DICKINSON
(1830–1886)

I dwell in Possibility —
A fairer House than Prose —
More numerous of Windows —
Superior — for Doors —

Of Chambers as the Cedars —
Impregnable of Eye —
And for an Everlasting Roof
The Gambrels of the Sky —

Of Visitors — the fairest —
For Occupation — This —
The spreading wide my narrow Hands
To gather Paradise —

The Brain — is wider than the Sky —
For — put them side by side —
The one the other will contain
With ease — and You — beside —

The Brain is deeper than the sea —
For — hold them — Blue to Blue —
The one the other will absorb —
As Sponges — Buckets — do —

The Brain is just the weight of God —
For — Heft them — Pound for Pound —
And they will differ — if they do —
As Syllable from Sound —

The Soul selects her own Society —
Then — shuts the Door —
To her divine Majority —
Present no more —

Unmoved — she notes the Chariots — pausing —
At her low Gate —
Unmoved — an Emperor be kneeling
Upon her Mat —

I've known her — from an ample nation —
Choose One —
Then — close the Valves of her attention —
Like Stone —

Some keep the Sabbath going to Church —
I keep it, staying at Home —
With a Bobolink for a Chorister —
And an Orchard, for a Dome —

Some keep the Sabbath in Surplice —
I just wear my Wings —
And instead of tolling the Bell, for Church,
Our little Sexton — sings.

God preaches, a noted Clergyman —
And the sermon is never long,
So instead of getting to Heaven, at last —
I'm going, all along.

My period had come for Prayer —
No other Art — would do —
My Tactics missed a rudiment —
Creator — Was it you?

God grows above — so those who pray
Horizons — must ascend —

And so I stepped upon the North
To see this Curious Friend —

His House was not — no sign had He —
By Chimney — nor by Door
Could I infer his Residence —
Vast Prairies of Air

Unbroken by a Settler —
Were all that I could see —
Infinitude — Had'st Thou no Face
That I might look on Thee?

The Silence condescended —
Creation stopped — for Me —
But awed beyond my errant —
I worshipped — did not "pray" —

I'm ceded — I've stopped being Theirs —
The name They dropped upon my face
With water, in the country church
Is finished using, now,
And They can put it with my Dolls,
My childhood, and the string of spools,
I've finished threading — too —

Baptized, before, without the choice,
But this time, consciously, of Grace —
Unto supremest name —
Called to my Full — The Crescent dropped —
Existence's whole Arc, filled up,
With one small Diadem.

My second Rank — too small the first —
Crowned — Crowing — on my Father's breast —
A half unconscious Queen —
But this time — Adequate — Erect,
With Will to choose, or to reject,
And I choose, just a Crown —

I felt a Funeral, in my Brain,
And Mourners to and fro
Kept treading — treading — till it seemed
That Sense was breaking through —

And when they all were seated,
A Service, like a Drum —
Kept beating — beating — till I thought
My Mind was going numb —

And then I heard them lift a Box
And creak across my Soul
With those same Boots of Lead, again,
Then Space — began to toll,

As all the Heavens were a Bell,
And Being, but an Ear,
And I, and Silence, some strange Race
Wrecked, solitary, here —

And then a Plank in Reason, broke,
And I dropped down, and down —
And hit a World, at every plunge,
And Finished knowing — then —

It might be lonelier
Without the Loneliness —
I'm so accustomed to my Fate —
Perhaps the Other — Peace —

Would interrupt the Dark —
And crowd the little Room —
Too scant — by Cubits — to contain
The Sacrament — of Him —

I am not used to Hope —
It might intrude upon —

Its sweet parade — blaspheme the place —
Ordained to Suffering —

It might be easier
To fail — with Land in Sight —
Than gain — My Blue Peninsula —
To perish — of Delight —

Me from Myself — to banish —
Had I Art —
Impregnable my Fortress
Unto All Heart —

But since Myself — assault Me —
How have I peace
Except by subjugating
Consciousness?

And since We're mutual Monarch
How this be
Except by Abdication —
Me — of Me?

Come slowly — Eden!
Lips unused to Thee —
Bashful — sip thy Jessamines —
As the fainting Bee —

Reaching late his flower,
Round her chamber hums —
Counts his nectars —
Enters — and is lost in Balms.

Wild Nights — Wild Nights!
Were I with thee

Wild Nights should be
Our luxury!

Futile — the Winds —
To a Heart in port —
Done with the Compass —
Done with the Chart!

Rowing in Eden —
Ah, the Sea!
Might I but moor — Tonight —
In Thee!

ROSALÍA DE CASTRO
(1837–1885)

They say that plants don't talk

They say that plants don't talk, nor do
   brooks or birds,
nor the wave with its chatter, nor stars
   with their shine.
They say it but it's not true, for whenever
   I walk by
they whisper and yell about me
           "There goes the crazy woman dreaming
of life's endless spring and of fields
and soon, very soon, her hair
   will be gray.
She sees the shaking, terrified frost
   cover the meadow."
There are gray hairs in my head; there is frost
   on the meadows,
but I go on dreaming—a poor, incurable
   sleepwalker—
of life's endless spring that is receding
and the perennial freshness of fields
   and souls.
although fields dry and souls burn up
Stars and brooks and flowers! Don't gossip about
   my dreams:
without them how could I admire you? How could
   I live?

(*translated by Aliki Barnstone and Willis Barnstone*)

ELSE LASKER-SCHÜLER
(1869–1945)

Abraham and Isaac

Abraham built a town of sod
and leaves in Eden's landscape
and practiced talking to his God.

Angels stopped in at his hut;
Abraham knew
the print left by each winged foot.

Until one day they heard the cries
of tortured goats:
little Isaac played at sacrifice.

And God called: Abraham! He broke
shells from the sea and coral rock
to decorate the altar on the bluff

and carried Isaac there, bound, on his back
to give the Lord His due.
The Lord, however, said: This is enough.

Jacob and Esau

Rebecca's maid: a girl come from afar,
an angel, lovely, in a shift of roses,
and on her face she seemed to wear a star.

Her eyes modestly lowered to her feet,
her soft hands sorted golden lentils,
baked bread and pottage with the meat.

The brothers thrived near her. They could
not quarrel over the sweets
that her sweet lap offered as food.

So Esau leaves the land for good,
leaves home and birthright for this meal.
The cloak he wears around his shoulders is the woods.

(*translated by Rosmarie Waldrop*)

YOSANO AKIKO
(1878–1942)

Spring quickly passes.
All the things of this world are
temporal! I cried,—
And lifted his hand to touch
my trembling, waiting breast.

In return for all
the sins and crimes of men,
the gods created me
with glistening long black hair
and pale, inviting skin.

It was only
the thin thread of a cloud,
almost transparent,
leading me along the way
like an ancient sacred song.

First Labor Pains

I am feeling bad today.
My body is feeling bad.
I am lying in bed before childbirth,
silent, with my eyes open.

Despite frequent brushes with death
and having gotten used to pain, blood, and screams,

why am I trembling with uncontrollable
anxiety and fear?

A young doctor consoled me and
told me about the happiness of birth.
I know it much better than he,
How useful is that now?

Knowledge does not belong to reality.
Experience belongs to the past.
Please, everyone, be quiet!
Would you remain as observers?

I am simply alone.
I am simply alone in heaven and on earth.
I will wait for my own act of God,
quietly biting my lip.

To give birth
is the only creation of truth
which actually explodes from within me.
There is no room for good and evil.

Now, the first labor pains . . .
The sun suddenly grows pale,
the world coldly calms down
and I am simply alone . . .

(*translated by Sam Hamill and Keiko Matsui Gibson*)

H.D.
(1886–1961)

from The Walls Do Not Fall

There is a spell, for instance,
in every sea-shell:

continuous, the sea thrust
is powerless against coral,

bone, stone, marble
hewn from within by that craftsman,

the shell-fish:
oyster, clam, mollusc

is master-mason planning
the stone marvel:

yet that flabby, amorphous hermit
within, like the planet

senses the finite,
it limits its orbit

of being, its house,
temple, fane, shrine:

it unlocks the portals
at stated intervals:

prompted by hunger,
it opens to the tide-flow:

but infinity? no,
of nothing-too-much:

I sense my own limit,
my shell-jaws snap shut

at invasion of the limitless,
ocean-weight; infinite water

can not crack me, egg in egg-shell;
closed in, complete, immortal

full-circle, I know the pull
of the tide, the lull

as well as the moon;
the octopus-darkness

is powerless against
her cold immortality;

so I in my own way know
that the whale

can not digest me:
be firm in your own small, static, limited

orbit and the shark-jaws
of outer circumstance

will spit you forth:
be indigestible, hard, ungiving,

so that, living within,
you beget, self-out-of-self,

selfless,
that pearl-of-great-price.

So, in our secretive, sly way,
we are proud and chary

of companionship with you others,
our betters, who seem to imply

that we will soon be swept aside,
crumpled rags, no good for banner-stuff,

no fit length for a bandage;
but when the shingles hissed

in the rain of incendiary,
other values were revealed to us,

other standards hallowed us;
strange texture, a wing covered us,

and though there was whirr and roar in the high air,
there was a Voice louder,

though its speech was lower
than a whisper.

Grant us strength to endure
a little longer,

now the heart's alabaster
is broken;

we would feed forever
on the amber honey-comb

of your remembered greeting,
but the old-self,

still half at-home in the world,
cries out in anger,

I am hungry, the children cry for food
and flaming stones fall on them;

our awareness leaves us defenceless;
O, for your Presence

among the fishing-nets
by the beached boats on the lake-edge;

when, in the drift of wood-smoke,
will you say again, as you said,

the baked fish is ready,
here is the bread?

Still the walls do not fall,
I do not know why;

there is zrr-hiss,
lightning in a not-known,

unregistered dimension;
we are powerless,

dust and powder fill our lungs
our bodies blunder

through doors twisted on hinges,
and the lintels slant

cross-wise;
we walk continually

on thin air
that thickens to a blind fog,

then step swiftly aside,
for even the air

is independable,
thick where it should be fine

and tenuous
where wings separate and open,

and the ether
is heavier than the floor,

and the floor sags
like a ship floundering;

we know no rule
of procedure,

we are voyagers, discoverers
of the not-known,

the unrecorded;
we have no map;

possibly we will reach haven,
heaven.

from Tribute to the Angels

We see her hand in her lap,
smoothing the apple-green

or the apple-russet silk;
we see her hand at her throat,

fingering a talisman
brought by a crusader from Jerusalem;

we see her hand unknot a Syrian veil
or lay down a Venetian shawl

on a polished table that reflects
half a miniature broken column;

we see her stare past a mirror
through an open window,

where boat follows slow boat on the lagoon;
there are white flowers on the water.

from The Flowering of the Rod

Blue-geese, white-geese, you may say,
yes, I know this duality, this double nostalgia;

I know the insatiable longing
in winter, for palm-shadow

and sand and burnt sea-drift;
but in the summer, as I watch

the wave till its edge of foam
touches the hot sand and instantly

vanishes like snow on the equator,
I would cry out, stay, stay;

then I remember delicate enduring frost
and its mid-winter dawn-pattern;

in the hot noon-sun, I think of the grey
opalescent winter-dawn; as the wave

burns on the shingle, I think,
you are less beautiful than frost;

but it is also true that I pray,
O, give me burning blue

and brittle burnt sea-weed
above the tide-line,

as I stand, still unsatisfied,
under the long shadow-on-snow of the pine.

So I would rather drown, remembering—
than bask on tropic atolls

in the coral-seas; I would rather drown
remembering—than rest on pine or fir-branch

where great stars pour down
their generating strength, Arcturus

or the sapphires of the Northern Crown;
I would rather beat in the wind, crying to these others:

yours is the more foolish circling,
yours is the senseless wheeling

round and round—yours has no reason—
I am seeking heaven;

yours has no vision,
I see what is beneath me, what is above me,

what men say is-not—I remember,
I remember, I remember—you have forgot:

you think, even before it is half-over,
that your cycle is at an end,

but you repeat your foolish circling—again, again, again;
again, the steel sharpened on the stone;

again, the pyramid of skulls;
I gave pity to the dead,

O blasphemy, pity is a stone for bread,
only love is holy and love's ecstasy

that turns and turns and turns about one centre,
reckless, regardless, blind to reality,

that knows the Islands of the Blest are there,
for *many waters can not quench love's fire.*

He was the first that flew
(the heavenly pointer)

but not content to leave
the scattered flock,

He journeys back and forth
between the poles of heaven and earth forever;

He was the first to wing
from that sad Tree,

but having flown, the Tree of Life
bears rose from thorn

and fragrant vine
from barren wood;

He was the first to say,
not to the chosen few,

his faithful friends,
the wise and good,

but to an outcast and a vagabond,
to-day shalt thou be with me in Paradise.

Anyhow, it is exactly written,
the house was filled with the odour of the ointment;

that was a little later and this was not such a small house
and was maybe already fragrant with boughs and wreaths,

for this was a banquet, a festival;
it was all very gay and there was laughter,

but Judas Iscariot turned down his mouth,
he muttered Extravagant under his breath,

for the nard though not potent,
had that subtle, indefinable essence

that lasts longer and costs more;
Judas whispered to his neighbour

and then they all began talking about the poor;
but Mary, seated on the floor,

like a child at a party, paid no attention;
she was busy; she was deftly un-weaving

the long, carefully-braided tresses
of her extraordinary hair.

MARIANNE MOORE
(1887–1972)

The Steeple-Jack

Dürer would have seen a reason for living
    in a town like this, with eight stranded whales
to look at; with the sweet sea air coming into your house
on a fine day, from water etched
    with waves as formal as the scales
on a fish.

One by one in two's and three's, the seagulls keep
    flying back and forth over the town clock,
or sailing around the lighthouse without moving their wings—
rising steadily with a slight
    quiver of the body—or flock
mewing where

a sea the purple of the peacock's neck is
    paled to greenish azure as Dürer changed
the pine green of the Tyrol to peacock blue and guinea
gray. You can see a twenty-five-
    pound lobster; and fish nets arranged
to dry. The

whirlwind fife-and-drum of the storm bends the salt
    marsh grass, disturbs stars in the sky and the
star on the steeple; it is a privilege to see so
much confusion. Disguised by what
    might seem the opposite, the sea-
side flowers and

trees are favored by the fog so that you have
    the tropics at first hand: the trumpet-vine.
fox-glove, giant snap-dragon, a salpiglossis that has

spots and stripes; morning-glories, gourds,
     or moon-vines trained on fishing-twine
at the back door;

cat-tails, flags, blueberries and spiderwort,
     striped grass, lichens, sunflowers, asters, daisies—
yellow and crab-claw ragged sailors with green bracts—toad-plant,
petunias, ferns; pink lilies, blue
     ones, tigers; poppies; black sweet-peas.
The climate

is not right for the banyan, frangipani, or
     jack-fruit trees; or for exotic serpent
life. Ring lizard and snake-skin for the foot, if you see fit;
but here they've cats, not cobras, to
     keep down the rats. The diffident
little newt

with white pin-dots on black horizontal spaced-
     out bands lives here; yet there is nothing that
ambition can buy or take away. The college student
named Ambrose sits on the hillside
     with his not-native books and hat
and sees boats

at sea progress white and rigid as if in
     a groove. Liking an elegance of which
the source is not bravado, he knows by heart the antique
sugar-bowl shaped summer-house of
     interlacing slats, and the pitch
of the church

spire, not true, from which a man in scarlet lets
     down a rope as a spider spins a thread;
he might be part of a novel, but on the sidewalk a
sign says C. J. Poole, Steeple-Jack,
     in black and white; and one in red
and white says

Danger. The church portico has four fluted
     columns, each a single piece of stone, made
modester by white-wash. This would be a fit haven for

waifs, children, animals, prisoners,
    and presidents who have repaid
sin-driven

senators by not thinking about them. The
    place has a school-house, a post-office in a
store, fish-houses, hen-houses, a three-masted
        schooner on
the stocks. The hero, the student,
    the steeple-jack, each in his way,
is at home.

It could not be dangerous to be living
    in a town like this, of simple people,
who have a steeple-jack placing danger-signs by the church
while he is gilding the solid-
    pointed star, which on a steeple
stands for hope.

ANNA AKHMATOVA
(1889–1966)

How can you look at the Neva

How can you look at the Neva,
how can you stand on the bridges? . . .
No wonder people think I grieve:
his image will not let me go.
Black angels' wings can cut one down,
I count the days till Judgment Day.
The streets are stained with lurid fires,
bonfires of roses in the snow.

(*translated by Stanley Kunitz with Max Hayward*)

Lot's Wife

The just man followed then his angel guide
Where he strode on the black highway, hulking and bright;
But a wild grief in his wife's bosom cried,
Look back, it is not too late for a last sight

Of the red towers of your native Sodom, the square
Where once you sang, the gardens you shall mourn,
And the tall house with empty windows where
You loved your husband and your babes were born

She turned, and looking on the bitter view
Her eyes were welded shut by mortal pain;
Into transparent salt her body grew,
And her quick feet were rooted in the plain.

Who would waste tears upon her? Is she not
The least of our losses, this unhappy wife?

Yet in my heart she will not be forgot
Who, for a single glance, gave up her life.

(translated by Richard Wilbur)

Until I collapse by the fence

Until I collapse by the fence
And the wind deals me the final blow,
The dream of salvation close at hand
Will burn me like an oath.

Stubborn, I wait for it to happen,
As a poem happens to me—
Confidently he will knock at the door
And, casual, cheerful, just as before,

He will enter and say: "Enough.
You see, I have forgiven too"—
It will not be frightful or painful . . .
Neither roses nor hosts of archangels.

So even in the frenzy of delirium
I spare my heart from torment,
For I cannot imagine death
Without this moment.

(August 30, 1921)

The Summer Garden

I want to visit the roses in that unique garden.
Fenced by the world's most magnificent fence.

Where the statues remember me as young,
And I remember them under the Neva's waters.

In the fragrant silence among majestic linden trees,
I imagine the creaking of masts of ships.

And the swan, as before, floats across centuries,
Admiring the beauty of its twin.

And sleeping there, like the dead, are hundreds of thousands of
    footsteps
Of friends and enemies, enemies and friends.

And the procession of shades is endless,
From the granite vase to the door of the palace.

My white nights whisper there
About some grand and mysterious love.

And everything glows like jasper and mother-of-pearl,
But the source of the light is mysteriously veiled.

July 9, 1959
Leningrad

(*translated by Judith Hemschemeyer*)

NELLY SACHS
(1891–1970)

Someone Is Alone

Someone is alone
is looking to the east
where melancholy shines in the face of dawn

Red is the east with cockcrow

O hear me—

To die
in the equator's
whipping lightning

O hear me—

To shrivel with the child faces of the cherubim
in the evening

O hear me—

In the blue north of the compass
waking at night
already a bud of death on the eyelids

now to the source—

(*translated by Willis Barnstone*)

White Snake

White snake
polar circle
wings in granite
rose sorrow in an ice-block
frontier zones around the secret
heart shaking miles of distance
chains of the wind hanging in homesickness
flaming hand grenade of anger—

And the snail
with the ticking suitcase of God time.

(translated by Aliki Barnstone and Willis Barnstone)

ALFONSINA STORNI
(1892–1938)

Lighthouse in the Night

The sky a black sphere,
the sea a black disk.

The lighthouse opens
its solar fan on the coast.

Spinning endlessly at night,
whom is it searching for

when the mortal heart
looks for me in my chest?

Look at the black rock
where it is nailed down.

A crow digs endlessly
but no longer bleeds.

My Sister

It's ten. Evening. The room is in half light.
My sister's sleeping, her hand on her chest; although
her face is very white, her bed entirely white,
the light, as if knowing, almost doesn't show.

She sinks into the bed the way pinkish fruit
does, into the deep mattress of soft grass.
Wind brushes her breasts, lifts them resolute-
ly chaste, measuring seconds as they pass.

I cover her tenderly with the white spread
and keep her lovely hands safe from the air.

On tiptoes I close all the doors near her bed,
leave the windows open, pull the curtain, prepare

for night. A lot of noise outside. Enough to drown
in: quarreling men, women with the juiciest
gossip. Hatred drifting upward, storekeepers shouting down
below. O voices, stop! Don't touch her nest.

Now my sister is weaving her silk cocoon
like a skillful worm. Her cocoon is a dream.
She weaves a pod with threads of a gold gleam.
Her life is spring. I am the summer afternoon.

She has only fifteen Octobers in her eyes
and so the eyes are bright, clear, and clean.
She thinks that storks from strange lands fly unseen,
leaving blond children with small red feet. Who tries

to come in? Is it you, now, the good wind?
You want to see her? Come in. But first cool
my forehead a second. Don't freeze the pool
of unwild dreams I sense in her. Undisciplined

they want to flood in and stay here, like you,
staring at that whiteness, at those tidy cheeks,
those fine circles under her eyes that speak
simplicity. Wind, you would see them and, falling to

your knees, cry. If you love her at all, be good
to her, for she will flee from wounding light.
Watch your word and intention. Her soul like wood
or wax is shaped, but rubbing makes a blight.

Be like that star which in the night stares at
her, whose eye is filtered through glassy thread.
That star rubs her eyelashes, turning like a cat
quiet in the sky, not to wake her in her bed.

Fly, if you can, among her snowy trees.
Pity her soul! She is immaculate.
Pity her soul! I know everything, but she's
like heaven and knows nothing. Which is her fate.

I Am Going to Sleep
(Suicide Poem)

Teeth of flowers, hairnet of dew,
hands of herbs, you, perfect wet nurse,
prepare the earthly sheets for me
and the down quilt of weeded moss.

I am going to sleep, my nurse, put me to bed.
Set a lamp at my headboard;
a constellation; whatever you like;
all are good: lower it a bit.

Leave me alone: you hear the buds breaking through . . .
a celestial foot rocks you from above
and a bird traces a pattern for you

so you'll forget . . . Thank you. Oh, one request:
if he telephones again
tell him not to keep trying, for I have left . . .

(translated by Aliki Barnstone and Willis Barnstone)

EDITH SÖDERGRAN
(1892–1923)

Two Goddesses

You were let down when you saw the face of happiness:
this sleeper with listless features,
most worshiped and talked about,
least known of all goddesses,
she who governs placid seas,
blooming gardens, endless days of sun,
and you vowed never to serve her.

Then sorrow again drew near with her deep eyes,
she who is never invoked,
best known and least understood of all goddesses,
she who governs stormy seas and sinking ships
and over those jailed for life
and over curses weighing on children in their mothers' wombs.

Vernal Mystery

My sister,
you come like a spring wind over our valleys . . .
Violets in shadow have the scent of fulfillment.
I want to take you to the loveliest place in the forest:
There we'll confess to each other how we saw God.

Instinct

My body is a mystery.
So long as this brittle thing lives
you will know its power.
I will save the world.

So Eros's blood surges through my lips
and Eros's gold through my tired hair.
I need only look
tired or hurting: the earth is mine.
When I lie on my bed, tired,
I know: in this tired hand is the fate of the earth.
Power quakes in my shoe,
power moves in the folds of my dress,
power, fearing no abyss, stands before you.

(translated by Aliki Barnstone and Willis Barnstone)

MARINA TSVETAYEVA
(1892–1941)

We shall not escape Hell

We shall not escape Hell, my passionate
sisters, we shall drink black resins—
we who sang our praises to the Lord
with every one of our sinews, even the finest,

we did not lean over cradles or
spinning wheels at night, and now we are
carried off by an unsteady boat
under the skirts of a sleeveless cloak,

we dressed every morning in
fine Chinese silk, and we would
sing our paradisal songs at
the fire of the robbers' camp,

slovenly needlewomen, (all
our sewing came apart), dancers,
players upon pipes: we have been
the queens of the whole world!

first scarcely covered by rags,
then with constellations in our hair, in
gaol and at feasts we have
bartered away heaven,

in starry nights, in the apple
orchards of Paradise.
—Gentle girls, my beloved sisters,
we shall certainly find ourselves in Hell!

1915

Bent with worry

Bent with worry, God
   paused, to smile.
And look, there were many
holy angels with bodies of

the radiance he had
   given them,
some with enormous wings and
others without any,

which is why I weep
   so much
because even more than God
himself I love his fair angels.

1916

from Verses about Moscow

Strange and beautiful brother—take this
city no hands built—out of my hands!

Church by church—all the forty times forty, and
the small pigeons also that rise over them.

Take the Spassky gate, with its flowers, where
the orthodox remove their caps, and

the chapel of stars, that refuge from evil,
where the floor is—polished by kisses.

Take from me the incomparable circle
of five cathedrals, ancient, holy friend!

I shall lead you as a guest from another
country to the Chapel of the Inadvertent Joy

where pure gold domes will begin to shine
for you, and sleepless bells will start thundering.

There the Mother of God will drop her
cloak upon you from the crimson clouds

and you will rise up filled with wonderful powers.
Then, you will not repent that you have loved me!

from Poems for Blok

You are going—west of the sun now.
You will see there—evening light.
You are going—west of the sun and
snow will cover up your tracks.

Past my windows—passionless
you are going in quiet snow.
Saint of God, beautiful, you
are the quiet light of my soul

but I do not long for your spirit.
Your way is indestructible.
And your hand is pale from holy
kisses, no nail of mine.

By your name I shall not call you.
My hands shall not stretch after you
to your holy waxen face I shall
only bow—from afar

standing under the slow falling snow, I shall
fall to my knees—in the snow.
In your holy name I shall only
kiss that evening snow

where, with majestic pace you
go by in tomb-like quiet,
the light of quiet—holy glory
of it: Keeper of my soul.

1916

Thinking him   human   they
decided to kill him, and
now he's dead. For ever.
—Weep. For the dead angel.

At the day's setting, he
sang the evening beauty.
Three waxen lights now
shudder superstitiously

and lines of light, hot
strings across the snow come from him.
Three waxen candles.
To the sun. The light-bearer.

O now look how
dark his eyelids are fallen,
O now look how
his wings are broken.

The black reciter reads.
The people idly stamp.
Dead lies the singer, and
celebrates resurrection.

1916

And the gadflies gather about indifferent cart-horses,
the red calico of Kaluga puffs out in the wind,
it is a time of whistling quails and huge skies,
bells waving over waves of corn, and more
talk about Germans than anyone can bear.
Now yellow, yellow, beyond the blue trees is a
cross, and a sweet fever, a radiance over
everything: your name   sounding like *angel*.

1916

Wherever you are I can reach you

Wherever you are I can reach you
to summon up—or send you back again!
Yet I'm no sorceress. My eyes grew sharp in
the white book—of that far-off river Don.

From the height of my cedar I see a world
where court decisions float, and all lights wander.
Yet from here I can turn the whole sea upside down
to bring you from its depths—or send you under!

You can't resist me, since I'm everywhere:
at daylight, underground, in breath and bread,
I'm always present. That is how I shall procure
your lips—as God will surely claim your soul—

in your last breath—and even in that choking hour
I'll be there, at the great Archangel's fence,
to put these bloodied lips up against the thorns
of Judgement—and to snatch you from your bier!

Give in! You must. This is no fairytale.
Give in! Any arrow will fall back on you.
Give in! Don't you know no one escapes
the power of creatures reaching out with

breath alone? (That's how I soar up
with my eyes shut and mica round my mouth . . .)
Careful, the prophetess tricked Samuel.
Perhaps I'll hoodwink you. Return alone,

because another girl is with you. Now on Judgement Day
there'll be no litigation. So till then
I'll go on wandering.
                    And yet I'll have your soul
as an alchemist knows how to win your

Lips . . .

1923

(*translated by Elaine Feinstein*)

MARINA TSVETAYEVA   153

ANONYMOUS HAWAIIAN

Dirge

I make this dirge for you Miss Mary Binning I miss you
o my daughter the wind of Na'alehu used to scatter dust in our house
o my daughter at the Lau-hu cliff
I'm crying for missing you and let it be; I love you I see us
o my daughter at the cold Ka-puna spring our water, in the rain
that the Ha'ao hill undergoes
up the trail almost nobody knew, us alone o my daughter
I'm missing you my life turns
a shade greyer forever
it's over now, you on your road endlessly who used to shine so my
   darling,
now in the one direction, away, me still in these places,
on a walk, up a hill, next to the spring dampening me, bent
from this stone yearning
                    o precious
as pearls, in Waikapuna the sun warmed you I didn't know you
from the flowers

(*translated by Armand Schwerner*)

ANONYMOUS INNUIT

Far Inland

Far inland
go my sad thoughts.
It is too much
never to leave this bench.
I want to wander
far inland.

I remember
hunting animals,
the good food.
It is too much
never to leave this bench.
I want to wander
far inland.

I hunted
like men. I earned
weapons, shot reindeer,
bull, cow, and calf,
killed them with my arrows
one evening
when almost winter
twilight fell
far inland.

I remember
how I struggled
inland
under the dropping sky
of snow.
The earth is white
far inland.

(*translated by Willis Barnstone, adapted from Knud Rasmussen*)

LORINE NIEDECKER
(1903–1970)

Hear
where her snow-grave is
the *You*
        ah you
of mourning doves

Swept snow, Li Po,
by dawn's 40-watt moon
to the road that hies to office
away from home.

Tended my brown little stove
as one would a cow—she gives heat.
Spring—marsh frog-clatter peace
            breaks out.

Tradition

[I]

The chemist creates
    the brazen
    approximation:
Life
    Thy will be done
    Sun

[II]

Time to garden
    before I
    die—

to meet
  my compost maker
  the caretaker
of the cemetery

Easter Greeting

I suppose there is nothing
so good as human
immediacy

I do not speak loosely
of handshake
              which is

              of the mind
or lilies—stand closer—
smell

BETTI ALVER
(B. 1906)

Iron Heaven

Today I saw a place no one has seen:
the heaven of the damned.
No one—proud or worried—goes
unharrassed by it
and it hammers on, endlessly. No one
escapes. No drought
can kill the coagulated petals
of its flowers.
Its horror:
what we did or longed to do
is perfect there.
On its oceans of glass no storm ages,
in its vineyards no pestilence rots.
The eternal fixed form
is open constantly. Never leaves
our glance.
My iron soul cracks
and finds the gold of heaven.
With no pride or worry
my iron soul shivers with the passion
of the earth
and feels its wings of weakness.

(*translated by Willis Barnstone and Felix Oinas*)

THÉRÈSE PLANTIER
(B. 1911)

Overdue Balance Sheet

Forgot to mail my letter to my friend Death
lost my pocketbook
took a lot of turns too sharply to the left
caught cold caught hot caught tepid caught fire caught nothing
skidded on an ice patch
had to chase from one place to another
parked
screwed up (got control in time)
hit the jackpot in matters of sheer idiocy
buried a cat I wrapped in the morning paper
was ashamed
was brave
was down and out
talked too much heard too much
tore my life to shreds
burned a hole in my pantsuit with a cigarette
and all at once caught sight of night.

(*translated by Maxine Kumin and Judith Kumin*)

MURIEL RUKEYSER
(1913–1980)

Waiting for Icarus

He said he would be back and we'd drink wine together
He said that everything would be better than before
He said we were on the edge of a new relation
He said he would never again cringe before his father
He said that he was going to invent full-time
He said he loved me that going into me
He said was going into the world and sky
He said all the buckles were very firm
He said the wax was the best wax
He said Wait for me here on the beach
He said Just don't cry.

I remember the gulls and the waves
I remember the islands going dark on the sea
I remember the girls laughing
I remember they said he only wanted to get away from me
I remember mother saying : Inventors are like poets,
                                        a trashy lot
I remember she told me those who try out inventions are worse
I remember she added : Women who love such are the worst of all
I have been waiting all day, or perhaps longer.
I would have liked to try those wings myself.
It would have been better than this.

JULIA DE BURGOS
(1914–1953)

Nothing

Since life is nothing in your philosophy,
let's drink to the fact of not being our bodies.

Let's drink to the nothing of your sensual lips,
which are sensual zeros in your blue kisses:
like all blue a chimerical lie
of white oceans and white firmaments.

Let's drink to the touchable decoy bird
sinking and rising in your carnal desire:
like all flesh, lightning, spark,
in the truth, unending lie of the universe.

Let's drink to nothing, the perfect nothing
of your soul, that races its lie on a wild colt:
like all nothing, perfect nothing, it's not even
seen for a second in sudden dazzle.

Let's drink to us, to them, to no one;
to our always nothing of our never bodies;
to everyone at least; to everyone so much nothing,
to bodiless shadows of the living who are dead.

We come from not being and march toward not being:
nothing between two nothings, zero between two zeros,
and since between two nothings nothing can be,
let's drink to the splendor of not being our bodies.

(*translated by Aliki Barnstone and Willis Barnstone*)

RUTH STONE

(B. 1915)

Green Apples

In August we carried the old horsehair mattress
To the back porch
And slept with our children in a row.
The wind came up the mountain into the orchard
Telling me something;
Saying something urgent.
I was happy.
The green apples fell on the sloping roof
And rattled down.
The wind was shaking me all night long;
Shaking me in my sleep
Like a definition of love,
Saying, this is the moment,
Here, now.

Finding Myself

Thursday, the 20th of July,
came to me and said,
I will give you this one elastic day.
Snap it shut or stretch it like bread dough.
So I put my hands in kneading and pulling.
It was a gauze-bag day.
The blue bell flower opened at the tip of its stalk.
I am a body not equipped to take every flag down hill,
but looking at all the exits and entrances,
I chose white wine in a plain glass goblet,
and wearing a flannel nightgown,
I went barefoot into the uncut grass.
The temperature rose.

The yeast began to work.
Every spider took to the air.
The cells of my skin puffed and tugged
and with a great shout let go their tethers
until looking up I saw myself like a cloud,
like ectoplasm, like an angel
among the branches of trees.
Then peeling layer after layer
I went to it letting go,
until only the elemental worm remained
letting itself down
on a string of spittle.

Once More

O my crows,
when you return in April,
your harsh voices,
your dark selves
rowing the raw air,
you males who made it home
to the mountain;
this shadow below you
in the orchard
is me,
triumphant,
listening
to rocks smash downstream
in the snowmelt.

The Mothers

Working out of mind, the wind says,
I take little or nothing.
I exchange one thing for another.
I rearrange.

Bother, the sand says,
she will not let me be,
slap, slap.

I cannot help it.
I have no bones of my own.
I am the mother of everything.
I am the lap of the world.
Dissolve in me, says the ocean.

We are the white eyes, sing the Himalayas.
We are the frozen cones of eternity.
We are the paradise of goats and tigers.
We hide the Abominable.
Only the wind,
only the melting snows
can wear us away grain by grain.
We are the land of the impossible.
We are the mothers of sand.

The sun flings her fiery hair
on the dark body of the universe.
Here are my offspring, she croons.
I will eat them all in time;
I will grow at one with my dark love—

the nothingness of nothing undefiled.
But they follow me like ducklings,
my piteous maimed little ones
with their cracked moons;
and my close, once perfect,
blue suffering child, ravaged.
I am the mother of sorrow.

The Plan

I said to myself, do you have a plan?
And the answer was always, no, I have no plan.
Then I would say to myself, you must think of one.
But what happened went on, chaotic with necessary pain.

During the winter the dogs dug moles from their runs
And rolled them blind on the frozen road.
Then the crossbills left at the equinox.
All this time I tried to think of a plan,
Something to bring the points together.
I saw that we move in a circle
But I was wordless in the field.
The smell of green steamed, everything shoved,
But I folded my hands and sat on the rocks.
Here I am, I said, with my eyes.
When they have fallen like marbles from their sockets,
What will become of this? And then I remembered
That there were young moles in my mind's eye,
Whose pink bellies shaded to mauve plush,
Whose little dead snouts sparkled with crystals of frost;
And it came to me, the blind will be leading the blind.

Look to the Future

To you born into violence,
the wars of the red ant are nothing;
you, in the heart of the eruption.

I am speaking from immeasurable grass blades.
You, there on the rubble,
what is the river of vapor to you?

You who are helpless as small birds
downed on the ice pack.
You who are spoiled as
commercial fruit by the medfly.

To you the machine guns.
To you the semen of fire,
the birth of the maggot in the corpse.

You, to whom we send these gifts;
at the heart of light we are crushed together.
When the sun dies we will become one.

ANNE HÉBERT
(B. 1916)

Life in the Castle

It is an ancestral castle
With no tables or fire
With no dust or rug

The perverse spell of this place
Is wholly in its shiny mirrors

The only possible thing to do here
Is to look at oneself day and night

Toss your image into the hard fountains
Your hardest image no shadow no color

See, these mirrors are deep
Like closets
Some corpse always lives there under the silver
Immediately covers your image
And sticks to you like seaweed.

It adjusts to you, skinny and naked,
And simulates love in a slow bitter shiver.

(*translated by Aliki Barnstone and Willis Barnstone*)

Bread Is Born

How do you make bread talk, this old treasure all wrapped
up in its strictures like a winter tree, anchored so that
its nakedness is set off against the see-through day?

If I lock myself up in the darkroom of my mind's eye
with this everlasting name stamped there, and if I importune
the old flat syllable to yield its shifting images

what I hear are a thousand blind and bitter animals thumping
against the door, a servile pack of hounds, slack and sub-
missive in their mangy pelts, who've been chomping on words
like grass since the dawn of time.

But a clean sweep of space stretches out for the poet,
an open field of wilderness and want, while on the far
side of the horizon time breaks open and the taste of
bread, salt, water sprouts like flat blue stones under the
sea. It's always like this, the age-old hunger.

Suddenly the hunger flows forth, it kneels on the ground,
it plants its round heart there in the shape of deep sleep.

O that long first night, face pressed against the cracked
earth, listening, taking the blood's pulse, all dream
banished, all movement arrested, all attention swelling to
love's tip.

The raw stubble pokes out of the land. An underground
source tells its green head of hair to break through.
The earth's belly bares its flowers and fruits in the
great noon sun.

The sky dusts itself blue; our stained hands flush with
the fields are like great fresh poppies.
All the shapes and colors that are called up from the
earth rise on the upbeat like a visible exhaled breath.

The land throbs and bleats. Its wool grows white under
the summer's jarring glare, the sour cicada song.

The millstones with their porous rough grains have the
muffled ardor of huge looking glasses condemned to reflect nothing.

All they can do is serve in the shadows, be heavy and
dark, hard and grating so as to shatter the heart of
the harvest, grind it to dust, to a stifling dry downpour.

It makes living flowers of these odd, pointy beach shells.
The seafaring sun crystallizes them in a bright spray. The
kernels open at once for us, singing, giving up their true,
well-crafted forms.

After that, we will sleek the milky dough, make it lie out
in its flat torpor, becalmed, still lacking breath where
it sleeps like a little pond.

And what if by chance the wind should rise? What if
our souls should give themselves up entirely? What if
their nights were clotted with roots, what if great holes
were bored in their days?

Even so, this bitter teaspoonful will outlast us, will
outlast all those who come after us. Crushed like October
leaves to release their musky smell, it will thrive in the
guise of yeast.

In the reek of roasted flesh, on the blackened stone, in
the midst of all this disorderly feasting, see how a pure
ancient act shines forth in the primal night. See how
that slow ripening of crust and dough heart begins while
Patience sits on the rim of the fire.

And nothing may touch its silence until morning.

Under the ashes which unmake themselves like a bed, watch
the round loaves and the square loaves puff up. Feel their
deep animal heat and the elusive heart perfectly centered
like a captive bird.

Oh, we live again! Day begins again at the skyline!
God can be born in His turn, a pale child to be put on
the cross in his season. Our work has already risen
brown and pungent with good smell.

We offer Him some bread for his hunger.

And in time we will sleep, heavy creatures, witness to
the festival and the drunkenness that morning catches us
in. And daylight straddles the world.

(*translated by Maxine Kumin*)

GWENDOLYN BROOKS
(B. 1917)

from The Children of the Poor

And shall I prime my children, pray, to pray?
Mites, come invade most frugal vestibules
Spectered with crusts of penitents' renewals
And all hysterics arrogant for a day.
Instruct yourselves here is no devil to pay.
Children, confine your lights in jellied rules;
Resemble graves; be metaphysical mules;
Learn Lord will not distort nor leave the fray.
Behind the scurryings of your neat motif
I shall wait, if you wish: revise the psalm
If that should frighten you: sew up belief
If that should tear: turn, singularly calm
At forehead and at fingers rather wise,
Holding the bandage ready for your eyes.

The Mother

Abortions will not let you forget.
You remember the children you got that you did not get,
The damp small pulps with a little or with no hair,
The singers and workers that never handled the air.
You will never neglect or beat
Them, or silence or buy with a sweet.
You will never wind up the sucking-thumb
Or scuttle off ghosts that come.
You will never leave them, controlling your luscious sigh,
Return for a snack of them, with gobbling mother-eye.

I have heard in the voices of the wind the voices of my dim
    killed children.

I have contracted. I have eased
My dim dears at the breasts they could never suck.
I have said, Sweets, if I sinned, if I seized
Your luck
And your lives from your unfinished reach,
If I stole your births and your names,
Your straight baby tears and your games,
Your stilted or lovely loves, your tumults, your marriages,
    aches, and your deaths,
If I poisoned the beginnings of your breaths,
Believe that even in my deliberateness I was not deliberate.
Though why should I whine,
Whine that the crime was other than mine?—
Since anyhow you are dead.
Or rather, or instead,
You were never made.
But that too, I am afraid,
Is faulty: oh, what shall I say, how is the truth to be said?
You were born, you had body, you died.
It is just that you never giggled or planned or cried.

Believe me, I loved you all.
Believe me, I knew you, though faintly, and I loved, I loved you
All.

Hunchback Girl: She Thinks of Heaven

My Father, it is surely a blue place
And straight. Right. Regular. Where I shall find
No need for scholarly nonchalance or looks
A little to the left or guards upon the
Heart to halt love that runs without crookedness
Along its crooked corridors. My Father,
It is a planned place surely. Out of coils,
Unscrewed, released, no more to be marvelous,
I shall walk straightly through most proper halls
Proper myself, princess of properness.

The Preacher: Ruminates Behind the Sermon

I think it must be lonely to be God.
Nobody loves a master. No. Despite
The bright hosannas, bright dear-Lords, and bright
Determined reverence of Sunday eyes.

Picture Jehovah striding through the hall
Of His importance, creatures running out
From servant-corners to acclaim, to shout
Appreciation of His merit's glare.

But who walks with Him?—dares to take His arm,
To slap Him on the shoulder, tweak His ear,
Buy Him a Coca-Cola or a beer,
Pooh-pooh His politics, call Him a fool?

Perhaps—who knows?—He tires of looking down.
Those eyes are never lifted. Never straight.
Perhaps sometimes He tires of being great
In solitude. Without a hand to hold.

The Rites for Cousin Vit

Carried her unprotesting out the door.
Kicked back the casket-stand. But it can't hold her,
That stuff and satin aiming to enfold her,
The lid's contrition nor the bolts before.
Oh oh. Too much. Too much. Even now, surmise,
She rises in the sunshine. There she goes,
Back to the bars she knew and the repose
In love-rooms and the things in people's eyes.
Too vital and too squeaking. Must emerge.
Even now she does the snake-hips with a hiss,
Slops the bad wine across her shantung, talks
Of pregnancy, guitars and bridgework, walks
In parks or alleys, comes haply on the verge
Of happiness, haply hysterics. Is.

The Chicago Defender Sends
a Man to Little Rock

Fall, 1957

In Little Rock the people bear
Babes, and comb and part their hair
And watch the want ads, put repair
To roof and latch. While wheat toast burns
A woman waters multiferns.

Time upholds or overturns
The many, tight, and small concerns.

In Little Rock the people sing
Sunday hymns like anything,
Through Sunday pomp and polishing.

And after testament and tunes,
Some soften Sunday afternoons
With lemon tea and Lorna Doones.

I forecast
And I believe
Come Christmas Little Rock will cleave
To Christmas tree and trifle, weave,
From laugh and tinsel, texture fast.

In Little Rock is baseball; Barcarolle.
That hotness in July . . . the uniformed figures raw and implacable
And not intellectual,
Batting the hotness or clawing the suffering dust.
The Open Air Concert, on the special twilight green. . . .
When Beethoven is brutal or whispers to lady-like air.
Blanket-sitters are solemn, as Johann troubles to lean
To tell them what to mean. . . .

There is love, too, in Little Rock. Soft women softly
Opening themselves in kindness,
Or, pitying one's blindness,
Awaiting one's pleasure
In azure

Glory with anguished rose at the root. . . .
To wash away old semi-discomfitures.
They re-teach purple and unsullen blue.
The wispy soils go. And uncertain
Half-havings have they clarified to sures.

In Little Rock they know
Not answering the telephone is a way of rejecting life,
That it is our business to be bothered, is our business
To cherish bores or boredom, be polite
To lies and love and many-faceted fuzziness.
I scratch my head, massage the hate-I-had.
I blink across my prim and pencilled pad.
The saga I was sent for is not down.
Because there is a puzzle in this town.
The biggest News I do not dare
Telegraph to the Editor's chair:
"They are like people everywhere."

The angry Editor would reply
In hundred harryings of Why.

And true, they are hurling spittle, rock,
Garbage and fruit in Little Rock.
And I saw coiling storm a-writhe
On bright madonnas. And a scythe
Of men harassing brownish girls.
(The bows and barrettes in the curls
And braids declined away from joy.)

I saw a bleeding brownish boy. . . .

The lariat lynch-wish I deplored.

The loveliest lynchee was our Lord.

GLORIA FUERTES
(B. 1918)

Interior Landscape

Like a madwoman and almost alone,
I take some food out to the country,
a thorn and foliage omelette
and a wine bag, while
I pull out a mulberry flute and play
a very green song of hope;
I see female turtledoves loving like male
    turtledoves,
a heron crossing the river
and through my thought crosses
a wingless "what is it to me?"

Human Geography

Look at my continent containing
arms, legs, and an unmeasured torso,
my feet are small, my hands tiny,
my eyes deep, my breasts pretty good.
I have a lake under my forehead
which at times spills over through the sockets
where it bathes the pupils of my eyes,
when crying gets into my legs
and my volcanoes quake in dance.

In the north I'm bordered by doubt
in the east by the other
in the west an Open Heart
and Castilian soil in the south.

Inside my continent there is content,
the united states of my body,

the state of pain at night,
the state of laughter in the soul—
state of the spinster all day long.

At noon I have earthquakes
if the wind of a letter doesn't reach me;
fire is furious and wipes out
the wheat harvest of my chest.
The forest of my poorly combed hair
stiffens when a river of blood
runs through the continent;
and not having sinned it pardons me.

The sea around me changes;
it's called Great Sea or Sea of People;
at times it shakes my sides,
at times it hugs me gently;
it depends on breezes or weather,
on heaven and cyclones maybe;

the fact is I'm an island
known to submerge or merge
in the waters of the human ocean
vulgarly known as the mob.

I've finished my lesson in geography.

Look at my contained continent.

(*translated by Willis Barnstone*)

MARY ELLEN SOLT

(B. 1920)

Forsythia

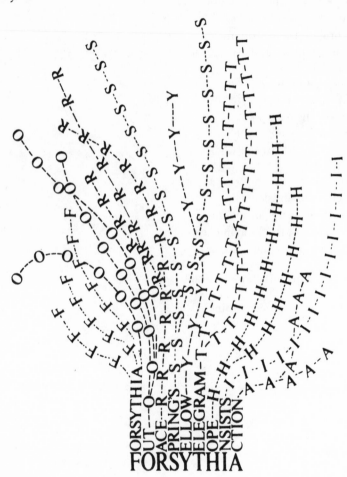

DENISE LEVERTOV
(1923–1998)

The Life of Others

Their high pitched baying
as if in prayer's unison

remote, undistracted, given over
utterly to belief,

the skein of geese
voyages south,
    hierarchic arrow of its convergence toward
    the point of grace
swinging and rippling, ribbon tail
of a kite, loftily

over lakes where they have not
elected to rest,

over men who suppose
earth is man's, over golden earth

preparing itself
for night and winter.
                We humans
are smaller than they, and crawl
unnoticed,

about and about the smoky map.

WISLAWA SZYMBORSKA
(B. 1923)

Lot's Wife

They say I looked back out of curiosity.
But I could have had other reasons.
I looked back mourning my silver bowl.
Carelessly, while tying my sandal strap.
So I wouldn't have to keep staring at the righteous nape
of my husband Lot's neck.
From the sudden conviction that if I dropped dead
he wouldn't so much as hesitate.
From the disobedience of the meek.
Checking for pursuers.
Struck by the silence, hoping God had changed his mind.
Our two daughters were already vanishing over the hilltop.
I felt age within me. Distance.
The futility of wandering. Torpor.
I looked back setting my bundle down.
I looked back not knowing where to set my foot.
Serpents appeared on my path,
spiders, field mice, baby vultures.
They were neither good nor evil now—every living thing
was simply creeping or hopping along in the mass panic.
I looked back in desolation.
In shame because we had stolen away.
Wanting to cry out, to go home.
Or only when a sudden gust of wind
unbound my hair and lifted up my robe.
It seemed to me that they were watching from the walls of Sodom
and bursting into thunderous laughter again and again.
I looked back in anger.
To savor their terrible fate.
I looked back for all the reasons given above.
I looked back involuntarily.

It was only a rock that turned underfoot, growling at me.
It was a sudden crack that stopped me in my tracks.
A hamster on its hind paws tottered on the edge.
It was then we both glanced back.
No, no. I ran on,
I crept, I flew upward
until darkness fell from the heavens
and with it scorching gravel and dead birds.
I couldn't breathe and spun around and around.
Anyone who saw me must have thought I was dancing.
It's not inconceivable that my eyes were open.
It's possible I fell facing the city.

On the Banks of the Styx

Dear individual soul, this is the Styx.
The Styx, that's right. Why are you so perplexed?
As soon as Charon reads the prepared text
over the speakers, let the nymphs affix
your name badge and transport you to the banks.
(The nymphs? They fled your woods and joined the ranks
of personnel here.) Floodlights will reveal
piers built of reinforced concrete and steel,
and hovercrafts whose beelike buzz resounds
where Charon used to ply his wooden oar.
Mankind has multiplied, has burst its bounds:
nothing, sweet soul, is as it was before.
Skyscrapers, solid waste, and dirty air:
the scenery's been harmed beyond repair.
Safe and efficient transportation (millions
of souls served here, all races, creeds, and sexes)
requires urban planning: hence pavilions,
warehouses, dry docks, and office complexes.
Among the gods it's Hermes, my dear soul,
who makes all prophecies and estimations
when revolutions and wars take their toll—
our boats, of course, require reservations.
A one-way trip across the Styx is free:
the meters saying, "No Canadian dimes,

no tokens" are left standing, as you see,
but only to remind us of old times.
From Section Thau Four of the Alpha Pier
you're boarding hovercraft Sigma Sixteen—
it's packed with sweating souls, but in the rear
you'll find a seat (I've got it on my screen).
Now Tartarus (let me pull up the file)
is overbooked, too—no way we could stretch it.
Cramped, crumpled souls all dying to get out,
one last half drop of Lethe in my phial . . .
Not faith in the beyond, but only doubt
can make you, sorry soul, a bit less wretched.

(*translated by Stanislaw Barańczak and Clare Cavanagh*)

I Am Too Near

I am too near to be dreamt of by him.
I do not fly over him, do not escape from him
under the roots of a tree. I am too near.
Not in my voice sings the fish in the net,
not from my finger rolls the ring.
I am too near. A big house is on fire
without me, calling for help. Too near
for a bell dangling from my hair to chime.
Too near to enter as a guest
before whom walls glide apart by themselves.
Never again will I die so lightly,
so much beyond my flesh, so inadvertently
as once in his dream. Too near.
I taste the sound, I see the glittering husk of this word
as I lie immobile in his embrace. He sleeps,
more accessible now to her, seen but once,
a cashier of a wandering circus with one lion,
than to me, who am at his side.
For her now in him a valley grows,
rusty-leaved, closed by a snowy mountain
in the dark blue air. I am too near

to fall to him from the sky. My scream
could wake him up. Poor thing
I am, limited to my shape,
I who was a birch, who was a lizard,
who would come out of my cocoons
shimmering the colors of my skins. Who possessed
the grace of disappearing from astonished eyes,
which is a wealth of wealths. I am near,
too near for him to dream of me.
I slide my arm from under the sleeper's head
and it is numb, full of swarming pins,
on the tip of each, waiting to be counted,
the fallen angels sit.

(*translated by Czeslaw Milosz*)

INGEBORG BACHMANN
(1926–1973)

You want the summer lightning

You want the summer lightning, throw the knives,
and tear the warm veins open to the air;

blinding you, the last fireworks soar,
soundlessly springing from the open pulses;

madness, contempt, then the revenge,
and already the remorse and disavowal.

You still notice how your blades get blunt,
and at long last you feel how love ends:

with honest thunderstorms and pure breath,
And in the dream dungeon it shuts you up.

Where its golden hair hangs down
you reach for it, the ladder into nothingness.

A thousand and one nights high are the rungs.
The step off into emptiness is the last step.

And where you rebound are the old places,
and every place you give three drops of blood.

Out of your mind, you hold rootless locks.
The bell rings, and it is enough.

The Firstborn Land

To my firstborn land, in the south,
I went and found, improverished and naked
and up to the waist in the sea,
town and castle.

Trodden by dust into sleep,
I lay in the light
and over me, leaved by Ionian salt,
a tree skeleton hung.

There fell no cream from it.

There blooms no rosemary,
no bird
refreshes its song in the springs.

In my firstborn land, in the south,
the viper sprang at me
and in the light, the horror.

O close,
close your eyes!
Press your mouth to the bite!

And as I drank myself
and the earthquake gently rocked
my firstborn land
I was woken up to seeing.

There life fell to me.

There stone is not dead.
The wick flares up
should a glance light it.

(*translated by Daniel Huws*)

Out of the corpse-warm vestibule of heaven steps the sun.
It is not the immortals who are there
but the war dead, so we understand.

And splendor pays no heed to decay. Our Godhead,
History, has ordained us a grave
from which there is no resurrection.

(*translated by Janice Orion*)

ANNE SEXTON
(1928–1974)

Somewhere in Africa

Must you leave, John Holmes, with the prayers and psalms
you never said, said over you? Death with no rage
to weigh you down? Praised by the mild God, his arm
over the pulpit, leaving you timid, with no real age,

whitewashed by belief, as dull as the windy preacher!
Dead of a dark thing, John Holmes, you've been lost
in the college chapel, mourned as father and teacher,
mourned with piety and grace under the University Cross.

Your last book unsung, your last hard words unknown,
abandoned by science, cancer blossomed in your throat,
rooted like bougainvillea into your gray backbone,
ruptured your pores until you wore it like a coat.

The thick petals, the exotic reds, the purples and whites
covered up your nakedness and bore you up with all
their blind power. I think of your last June nights
in Boston, your body swollen but light, your eyes small

as you let the nurses carry you into a strange land.
. . . If this is death and God is necessary let him be hidden
from the missionary, the well-wisher and the glad hand.
Let God be some tribal female who is known but forbidden.

Let there be this God who is a woman who will place you
upon her shallow boat, who is a woman naked to the waist,
moist with palm oil and sweat, a woman of some virtue
and wild breasts, her limbs excellent, unbruised and chaste.

Let her take you. She will put twelve strong men at the oars
for you are stronger than mahogany and your bones fill

the boat high as with fruit and bark from the interior.
She will have you now, you whom the funeral cannot kill.

John Holmes, cut from a single tree, lie heavy in her hold
and go down that river with the ivory, the copra and the gold.

July 1, 1962.

Not So. Not So.

I cannot walk an inch
without trying to walk to God.
I cannot move a finger
without trying to touch God.
Perhaps it is this way:
He is in the graves of the horses.
He is in the swarm, the frenzy of the bees.
He is in the tailor mending my pantsuit.
He is in Boston, raised up by the skyscrapers.
He is in the bird, that shameless flyer.
He is in the potter who makes clay into a kiss.

Heaven replies:
Not so! Not so!

I say thus and thus
and heaven smashes my words.

Is not God in the hiss of the river?

Not so! Not so!

Is not God in the ant heap,
stepping, clutching, dying, being born?

Not so! Not so!

Where then?
I cannot move an inch.

Look to your heart
that flutters in and out like a moth.

God is not indifferent to your need.
You have a thousand prayers
but God has one.

As It Was Written

Earth, earth,
riding your merry-go-round
toward extinction,
right to the roots,
thickening the oceans like gravy,
festering in your caves,
you are becoming a latrine.

Your trees are twisted chairs.
Your flowers moan at their mirrors,
and cry for a sun that doesn't wear a mask.

Your clouds wear white,
trying to become nuns
and say novenas to the sky.
The sky is yellow with its jaundice,
and its veins spill into the rivers
where the fish kneel down
to swallow hair and goat's eyes.

All in all, I'd say,
the world is strangling.
And I, in my bed each night,
listen to my twenty shoes
converse about it.
And the moon,
under its dark hood,
falls out of the sky each night,
with its hungry red mouth
to suck at my scars.

Mary's Song

Out of Egypt
with its pearls and honey,
out of Abraham, Isaac, Jacob,
out of the God I AM,
out of the diseased snakes,
out of the droppings of flies,
out of the sand dry as paper,
out of the deaf blackness,
I come here to give birth.

Write these words down.
Keep them on the tablet of miracles.
Withdraw from fine linen and goat's hair
and be prepared to anoint yourself with oil.
My time has come.
There are twenty people in my belly,
there is a magnitude of wings,
there are forty eyes shooting like arrows,
and they will all be born.
All be born in the yellow wind.

I will give suck to all
but they will go hungry,
they will go forth into suffering.
I will fondle each
but it will come to nothing.
They will not nest
for they are the Christs
and each will wave good-bye.

SYLVIA PLATH

(1932–1963)

Crossing the Water

Black lake, black boat, two black, cut-paper people.
Where do the black trees go that drink here?
Their shadows must cover Canada.

A little light is filtering from the water flowers.
Their leaves do not wish us to hurry:
they are round and flat and full of dark advice.

Cold worlds shake from the oar.
The spirit of blackness is in us, it is in the fishes.
A snag is lifting a valedictory, pale hand;

Stars open among the lilies.
Are you not blinded by such expressionless sirens:
This is the silence of astounded souls.

4 April 1962

The Moon and the Yew Tree

This is the light of the mind, cold and planetary.
The trees of the mind are black. The light is blue.
The grasses unload their griefs on my feet as if I were God,
Prickling my ankles and murmuring of their humility.
Fumy, spiritous mists inhabit this place
Separated from my house by a row of headstones.
I simply cannot see where there is to get to.

The moon is no door. It is a face in its own right,
White as a knuckle and terribly upset.
It drags the sea after it like a dark crime; it is quiet

With the O-gape of complete despair. I live here.
Twice on Sunday, the bells startle the sky——
Eight great tongues affirming the Resurrection.
At the end, they soberly bong out their names.

The yew tree points up. It has a Gothic shape.
The eyes lift after it and find the moon.
The moon is my mother. She is not sweet like Mary.
Her blue garments unloose small bats and owls.
How I would like to believe in tenderness——
The face of the effigy, gentled by candles,
Bending, on me in particular, its mild eyes.

I have fallen a long way. Clouds are flowering
Blue and mystical over the face of the stars.
Inside the church, the saints will be all blue,
Floating on their delicate feet over the cold pews,
Their hands and faces stiff with holiness.
The moon sees nothing of this. She is bald and wild.
And the message of the yew tree is blackness—blackness and silence.

22 October 1961

Edge

The woman is perfected.
Her dead

Body wears the smile of accomplishment,
The illusion of a Greek necessity

Flows in the scrolls of her toga,
Her bare

Feet seem to be saying:
We have come so far, it is over.

Each dead child coiled, a white serpent,
One at each little

Pitcher of milk, now empty.
She has folded

Them back into her body as petals
Of a rose close when the garden

Stiffens and odors bleed
From the sweet, deep throats of the night flower.

The moon has nothing to be sad about,
Staring from her hood of bone.

She is used to this sort of thing.
Her blacks crackle and drag.

INGRID JONKER
(1933–1965)

This Journey

This journey that obliterates your image
torn blood-angel thrown to the dogs
this landscape is deserted as my forehead
Wound of the roses

How I wanted to see you walk without chains
I longed to see your face open and free
your broken face dead and dry as the mud
Wound of the earth

In the nights of absence without eyes
I cried to see a real star in your hand
I cried to see the blue sky and to hear
One word from life

Bitter angel untrue with a flame in your mouth
under your armpits I have placed two swallows
and drawn a secret cross on your face
For the man

of whom you reminded me once

(*translated by Jack Cope and William Plomer*)

LUCILLE CLIFTON
(B. 1936)

anna speaks of the childhood
of mary her daughter

we rise up early and
we work. work is the medicine
for dreams.
             that dream
i am having again;
she washed in light,
whole world bowed to its knees,
she on a hill looking up,
face all long tears.
             and shall i give her up
to dreaming then? i fight this thing.
all day we scrubbing   scrubbing.

holy night

joseph, i afraid of stars,
their brilliant seeing.
so many eyes. such light.
joseph, i cannot still these limbs,
i hands keep moving toward i breasts,
so many stars. so bright.
joseph, is wind burning from east
joseph, i shine, oh joseph,   oh
illuminated night.

leda 1

there is nothing luminous
about this.
they took my children.
i live alone in the backside
of the village.
my mother moved
to another town. my father
follows me around the well,
his thick lips slavering,
and at night my dreams are full
of the cursing of me
fucking god fucking me.

slaveships

loaded like spoons
into the belly of Jesus
where we lay for weeks for months
in the sweat and stink
of our own breathing
Jesus
why do you not protect us
chained to the heart of the Angel
where the prayers we never tell
and hot and red
as our bloody ankles
Jesus
Angel
can these be men
who vomit us out from ships
called Jesus   Angel   Grace Of God
onto a heathen country
Jesus
Angel
ever again
can this tongue speak
can these bones walk
Grace Of God
can this sin live

david, musing

it was i who faced the lion and the bear
who gathered the five smooth stones
and the name of the first was hunger
and the name of the second was faith
and the name of the third was lyric
and passion the fourth and the fifth
was the stone of my regret   it was hunger
that brought the gore of the giant's head
into my hand
the others i fastened under my tongue
for later   for her   for israel   for my sons

what manner of man

if i am not singing to myself
to whom then?   each sound, each word
is a way of wondering that first
brushed against me in the hills
when i was an unshorn shepherd boy.
each star that watched my watching then
was a mouth that would not speak.

what is a man? what am i?

even when i am dancing now i am dancing
myself onto the tongue of heaven
hoping to move into some sure
answer from the Lord.
how can this david love himself,
be loved (i am singing and spinning now)
if he stands in the tents of history
bloody skull in one hand, harp in the other?

BELLA AKHMADULINA
(B. 1937)

In the Emptied Rest Home

To fall, like an apple, no mind,
no memory! To lie
on the soft ground, blank as an apple,
to not feel this body.

An apple: muscles of moisture,
veins of color, all sorts of changes
crowding each other out.
The apple doesn't care.

Hopeless to care here,
it's war, whole gangs of orphans
run wild with real guns and knives,
and the water's rising.

And it's boring. I'm tired of looking at it
both ways, doctor and patient.
The same crackling heart, the same
tickling run of the molecules.

I'm ready to turn away,
but I don't turn away: I half stay,
the way you half listen to someone
whistling in the next apartment.

Solitude, distance. The snow keeps on rising
up on the roof. I'm too much alone,
it's as if there were two of us here,
the air in my lungs, the beat in my blood.

But my eyes can still see, my voice
squeaks, my pulse beats like a moth

in my closed hand: oh, thank God, my body,
little child, little mouse! Thank God

there's something alive in this house!
In the dead of winter, alone,
go on with your simple life, the life
of the black woods, the vegetable gardens, the sun.

(translated by Jean Valentine and Olga Carlisle)

LINDA GREGG
(B. 1942)

God's Places

Does the soul care about the mightiness
of this love? No. The soul is a place
and love must find its way there.
A fisherman on his boat swung a string
of fish around his head and threw it
across the water where it landed at my feet.
That was a place. One day I walked into
a village that was all ruins. It was noon.
Nobody was there, the roofs were gone,
the silence was heavy. A man came out,
gradually other people, but no one spoke.
Then somebody gave me a glass of water
with a lump of jam on a spoon in it.
It was a place, one of God's places,
but love was not with me. I breathed
the way grape vines live and give in
to the whole dream of being and not being.
The soul must be experienced to be achieved.
If you love me as much as you say you
love me, stay. Let us make a place
of that ripeness the soul speaks about.

Slow Dance by the Ocean

The days are hot and moist now. The doves say
true, true, true and fly lovely all the time
from and to the tree outside my window,
not quieted by the weather as the cats are.
The dogs bark only when there is a stranger.

The world moves, my Lord, and I stay still,
yielding as it passes through. I go down
the path to a bay that holds the ocean quiet,
a grassy place with oleander and broom.
When evening comes, things are clear delicately
until all is dark except the water, which is silver.
The sea takes me at night while I sleep.
During the day, memory is the pull of its huge
center. I have my dress to wash and lamps to clean
in the coming and going of time. I dance as slowly
as possible in the fields of barley and weeds.

In Dirt under Olive Trees on the Hill at Evening

Her naked body is too small for the woman's head.
The face tilts away as it listens to the music
She makes, the expression perfect happiness.
A diadem and curly hair with bits of gold
and white and red paint. The only wing left
curves from Her shoulder like the tail of a horse
prancing. Why do we care so much about the grace
of winged women, singing naked or lightly clothed?
Made by men to what purpose? A rock would do
as well, or some broken weeds. Why not the smell
of earth warmed all day by the sun, or the sense
of unseen water underground, or the sky at morning?
Why this pity, this glad humming when we see Her
sitting with tinted breasts on a little clay throne?

All the Spring Lends Itself to Her

If Her skirt does not bend the grass, nor sea air
mold Her shape while She is happy, there is no grace.
I will not stop looking for that. Song and color
circle in this air for Her to stand in.
If She does not come to take pleasure in this giving,
all things will reverse to alms and penitence.
She is not needed for this world to be a success.

Either way the other powers will have their time.
But if spring comes and She is absent, we will eat
food without sacrament, our hearts not renewed
for the other seasons: the one where we give, the one
where we are taken, and the season where we are lost
in the darkness. If love does not reign,
we are unsuited for the season of ripeness.
If we do not see Her body in the glass of this beauty,
the sun will blind us. We will lie in the humming fields
and call to Her, coaxing Her back. We will lie
pressed close to the earth, calling Her name,
wondering if it is Her voice we are whispering.

A Flower No More than Itself

She was there on the mountain,
still as the fig tree and the failed wheat.
Only the lizards and a few goats moved.
Everything stunned by heat and silence.
I would get to the top of the terraced starkness
with my ankles cut by thistles and all of me
drained by the effort in the fierce light.
I would put the pomegranate and the anise
and a few daisies on the great rock
where the fountain was long ago.
Too tired to praise. And found each time
tenderness and abundance in the bareness.
Went back down knowing I would sleep clean.
That She would be awake all year with sun
and dirt and rain. Pride Her life.
All nature Her wealth. Sound of owls Her pillow.

JENI COUZYN
(B. 1942)

Spell for Jealousy

Be loved, my beloved.
Be sweetened, sour one.
Be filled, empty one.

Bring all the thief has given home to our house
Bring all the thief has given home to our bed
Bring all the thief has given home to our love
Bring all the thief has given home to me.

Light of her brighten me
Spite of her strengthen me
Joy of her gladden me.

Lady as candle is to the full sun of noon
As toad is to the great whale of the ocean
As leaf is to the mighty forest of the mountain
Are you now to me and my loved one.

Let the wind take you
Let the water take you
Let the rain take you

You are burr in his sock
You are grain in his shoe
Now he will forget you.

Creation

You were made
under the sea
your ear gives you away.

You were made
in the calyx of a rose
your skin betrays you.

You were made in heaven
your eyelids as you sleep
cannot disguise themselves.

You were brought to me
by a giant kite
his wings stir white

on my face still.
Never say you grew
from a seed in my body

the dandelion brought you
the spring brought you
a star with brilliant hands

delivered you
leaving his light in your eyes
as a seal, and a promise.

TESS GALLAGHER
(B. 1943)

Wake

Three nights you lay in our house.
Three nights in the chill of the body.
Did I want to prove how surely
I'd been left behind? In the room's great dark
I climbed up beside you onto our high bed, bed
we'd loved in and slept in, married
and unmarried.

There was a halo of cold around you
as if the body's messages carry farther
in death, my own warmth taking on the silver-white
of a voice sent unbroken across snow just to hear
itself in its clarity of calling. We were dead
a little while together then, serene
and afloat on the strange broad canopy
of the abandoned world.

LOUISE GLÜCK
(B. 1943)

Mythic Fragment

When the stern god
approached me with his gift
my fear enchanted him
so that he ran more quickly
through the wet grass, as he insisted,
to praise me. I saw captivity
in praise; against the lyre,
I begged my father in the sea
to save me. When
the god arrived, I was nowhere,
I was in a tree forever. Reader,
pity Apollo: at the water's edge,
I turned from him, I summoned
my invisible father—as
I stiffened in the god's arms,
of his encompassing love
my father made
no other sign from the water.

YONA WALLACH
(1944–1985)

Never Will I Hear the Sweet Voice of God

Never will I hear the sweet voice of God
never again will his sweet voice pass under my window
big drops will fall in the wide open spaces a sign
God doesn't come anymore through my window
how again will I see his sweet body
dive into his eye not descend anymore to pull out
glances that pass by in the universe like wind
how will I remember this beauty and not weep
days will pass in my life like spasms in the body
near shards of touch remembered shattered from weeping
the form of his motion when he moves enchanting the air
never will the voice of longing pass the threshold
when man will revive like the dead in memory, like being
if only his sweet glance would stand by my bed and I weep.

Not a Man
Not a Woman

Not a man
not a woman
make love
bare breasts
without a visage
sex and face
like in Kabbala
in black magic
the inside peels off
they lose the
face
not a man

not a woman
in the face
a feeling dead
in sex organs
the sensation
the brain filled with
good will
but more
with fear
yet possible to preserve
the emotional
virginity
until the messiah comes
and he will come
the woman will be woman
the man man
their faces sexual
and in their limbs sense
will be resurrected
a white turtle
a great wall
that from a wave became
a dam for all feeling
which breaks up like
a cascade
to drown the woman man
and man woman

(*translated by Linda Zisquit*)

LINDA HOGAN
(B. 1947)

Guarding a Child's Sleep

Her body sweats in sleep
as if red fire entered her mouth
burning to speak,
exiling dreams
into the tense narrow bone of shoulder,
the black tangle of hair.

That life at night,
the life of a fisherman
sending hooks out
and reeling them in, empty.
Empty nets.

But she has not given in.
Even the taut muscles are working
to shape the woman's body.
The lace of nerves unravel
like a comet's tail.

Multitudes are suspended in her face,
the eyes of an unknown grandfather,
black eyes looking like turmoil
behind a closed door.

I would like to dream for her
a paradise of sudden flowers
breaking open a skein of light
but all the words I whisper
are people traveling
who lost their way
who lost their red horses
as if tethered to fire.

OLGA BROUMAS
(B. 1949)
and T BEGLEY
(B. 1956)

from Sappho's Gymnasium

this helpless desire your own suffering the
work of grace makes us visible
flocking on small
islands of inland waters the near
shore of unsayable

the lamp stands on the little table
and the little table is spread the bed
is a prayer and here is this room in a near
dead darkness in which I first
know you undo the garden of exceeding
happiness after each flush I
end up crying
after the ships
called bluets and innocents

grief that is not expressed I have saved
and at times recovering my natural
voice I sit by the death bed she is
so beautiful a transparence one speaks
is the beginning of
memory of sensation let me make
it good light being unborn

What if there were no sea
to take up the table of our hearts
breath which is everywhere curved
hand from infinity broken

Peaceful limbs
had been little breathless
branches of two humans
the gods are open mouthed

By long kiss the icon is
worn a lighter color
than the rest of the face
bathing the living

I don't know virgin
when I was made I was made

I come single
alone
under my clothes

Desert silence
who must constantly beat her wings

Transitive body this fresco amen I mouth

You feel the bruising midflight as one born
to dazzle god with your heat
beside me on the bed your foot
taken into my mouth
I tongue the injured core of its birthright
and the hot burning off of self which exhausts it

I have procreated
unless writing
studies the image
and no more

Where I unbind my hair light's first blue witness

Like flocks of solitudes surrender
a bird beautiful and uncovered
I bite small seas into your heart
populate with birds a sky
immaculate with shriek of wing
for its updraft I have married

I am not alone
facing the sun
lover of all

Among indelible black
cosmos I keep words
or sing

Wonderful mineral like lemon being eaten
in my gums lucid saliva
your translated trance I am performing it
asylum through my clearest my solid birthright
   singing
full time mercy break god.

I didn't cover myself
I looked instead right back

Art is climax over conduct
zen of no color by sunrise I do

Here at the threshold we took off our cloths
and though I don't remember everything I remember
   the place
I first saw death seeking a wound and since then
   one other
sensually nothing I can by now recognize an injection
   of sleep
spinning clobbered with substance
willing to be sung

There is no way of rainbow for looking eye is broke
child behind unknown tongue

Give me your hand candidate for the light
the light won't wake you
nor the fragrant wetting just begun
to join the litany of the visible
we go in and out of the lung

Sprig then when stronger leaf
I lie all night with her
I live where she is many
committing cleanness
the chosen chemical suffusing the harm
to the end of helping city
I'm on the side of I spread myself around
I look forward to it
I get on my knees

On the way to clearest practice the one I want takes my
    offering
unaided rose outside the chapel
gigantic in the unfurled song
under her feet the prows
of boats in the stilltide

I dream in the land
I lose all sensation
I last an instant
dazzling altar
angels and angels
one church.

Lord let me all I can wild cherry
I'm dazed all my ways of arriving bear tracks
failure of being torn to pieces is me
mumbling anxiety and I love my heart
I do each day lightly suffering desire
for kindness vividly today
idiot red unselfish green blue threadbare of cloud
outside the labyrinth imagining my life

Insistent love I won't outlive the words I lamb in your
   mouth
anachrist of the bewildered touch of extreme hands

The soul has a knee
just risen just rinses

Laurel to air I speak your lips
lantern in the abyss

I am what astonishment can bear
tongue I owe you

Pupil only to you
fleece of dew

LILIANA URSU
(B. 1949)

The Moon

Proud breast in the chill nucleus of the night,
illusion through which I make confession to autumn.
No one knows you better than this poplar,
this vacant plot of earth,
this hyacinth,
this telephone.

You are an orange tree draped in snow,
a mask abandoned in the sky,
cotton candy hawked at the fair of the human condition,
a wheelchair for an angel
or maybe an immense balloon.
The earth, invisibly attached, is your gondola-car,
weighing you down.

O moon, o bored mystery.

(*translated by Liliana Ursu, Adam J. Sorkin, and Tess Gallagher*)

ANNE CARSON
(B. 1950)

from The Truth about God

GOD'S NAME

God had no name.
Isaac had two names.
Isaac was also called The Blind.

Inside the dark sky of his mind
Isaac could hear God
moving down a country road bordered by trees.

By the way the trees reflected off God
Isaac knew which ones were straight and tall
or when they carried their branches

as a body does its head
or why some crouched low to the ground in thickets.
To hear how God was moving through the universe

gave Isaac his question.
I could tell you his answer
but it wouldn't help.

The name is not a noun.
It is an adverb.
Like the little black notebooks that Beethoven carried

in his coatpocket
for the use of those who wished to converse with him,
the God adverb

is a one-way street that goes everywhere you are.
No use telling you what it is.
Just chew it and rub it on.

from Book of Isaiah

[III]

Isaiah walked for three years in the valley of vision.

In his jacket of glass he crossed deserts and black winter mornings.

The icy sun lowered its eyelids against the glare of him.

God stayed back.

Now Isaiah had a hole in the place where his howl had broken off.

All the while Isaiah walked, Isaiah's heart was pouring out the hole.

One day Isaiah stopped.

Isaiah put his hand on the amputated place.

Isaiah's heart is small but in a way sacred, said Isaiah, I will save it.

Isaiah plugged the hole with millet and dung.

God watched Isaiah's saving action.

God was shaking like an olive tree.

Now or never, whispered God.

God reached down and drew a line on the floor of the desert in front
   of Isaiah's feet.

Silence began.

Silence roared down the canals of Isaiah's ears into his brain.

Isaiah was listening to the silence.

Deep under it was another sound Isaiah could hear miles down.

A sort of ringing.

Wake up Isaiah! said God from behind Isaiah's back.

Isaiah jumped and spun around.

Wake up and praise God! said God smiling palely.

Isaiah spat.

God thought fast.

The nation is burning! God cried pointing across the desert.

Isaiah looked.

All the windows of the world stood open and blowing.

In each window Isaiah saw a motion like flames.

Behind the flames he saw a steel fence lock down.

Caught between the flames and the fence was a deer.

Isaiah saw the deer of the nation burning all along its back.

In its amazement the deer turned and turned and turned

until its own shadow lay tangled around its feet like melted wings.

Isaiah reached out both his hands, they flared in the dawn.

Poor flesh! said Isaiah.

Your nation needs you Isaiah, said God.

Flesh breaks, Isaiah answered. Everyone's will break. There is nothing
we can do.

I tell you Isaiah you can save the nation.

The wind was rising, God was shouting.

You can strip it down, start over at the wires, use lions! use thunder!
use what you see—

Isaiah was watching sweat and tears run down God's face.

Okay, said Isaiah, so I save the nation. What do *you* do?

God exhaled roughly.

I save the fire, said God.

Thus their contract continued.

DEBORAH DIGGES
(B. 1950)

Winter Barn

A light slant snow dragging the fields, a counter-wind
where the edges of the barn frayed worlds,

blurred outside in. This is what my love could give me
instead of children—the dusk as presence, moth-like,

and with a moth's dust colored flickering stall by stall,
some empty now, certain gone to slaughter, driven north

in open trucks over pot-holed, frozen roads.
Such a hard ride to blood-let, blankness, the stalls' stone

floors hosed out, yet damp, the urine reek not quite
muffled with fresh hay, trough water still giving back lantern

light like ponds at nightfall. Sheep lay steaming, cloud
in cloud. The barn cat slept among last summer's lambs, black

faced, apart, relieved of their mothers. We made our way,
my dogs and I, to say hello to the Yorkshire sow

named Kora, who heaved herself up to greet us,
let the dogs lick her oiled snout smeared with feed,

while I scratched her forehead. Kora of the swineherds
fallen with Persephone, perhaps in hell a bride's only company.

Prodigal, planetary, Kora's great spined, strict bristled body
wore the black mud of a cold, righteous creation,

burs and mugwort plastered at the gates.
Days her smell stayed with us. The last time we saw her

the plaque bearing her name was gone. Maybe she would be mated.
Sparrows sailed the barn's doomed girth, forsaken,

therefore free. They lit on rafters crossing the west windows
that flared at sunset like a furnace fed on stars.

Lilacs

Let's say for that time
I was an instrument forbidding music.
That spring no thief of fire.
I tapped from the source a self sick of love,
and then beyond sickness,
an invalid of my loathing.
Yes, loathing put me to bed each night
and burned my dreams,
in the morning woke me with strong coffee.
And this was loathing's greeting—
Get up. Drink.
All this in spite of the lilacs returning,
their odor the odor of life everlasting,
another year,
another season onward, another spring.
But they bloomed of a sudden pale in unison
like lifeboats rowing into dawn,
the passengers gone mad in their exhaustion in the open,
even the wives, even the mothers
rescued for their children,
their lives, believe me, not their own.
Boats full of lilacs drifting thus,
each greyish bush against my grey house.
But theirs is a short season, a few weeks,
rarely more.
And I was glad to be rid of them,
Rid of a thing that could touch in me
what might be called "mercy".
See how one's lips must kiss to make the *m*,
touch tongue to back of teeth and smile.
Pity's swept clean and conscious,
an upstairs room whose floors resound,
but mercy's an asylum,
a house sliding forever out to sea.

As if I were expected to wade out into the yard each night
and swing a lantern!
And just this morning still early into autumn
I noticed how the lilacs had set themselves on fire.
As for me, I have my privacy.
It's mine I might have killed for.
I have my solitude,
the face of the beloved like a room locked in time
and when I look back I am not there.
It's as if the lilacs martyred themselves,
the stories of their journey
embellished or misread
or lacking a true bard, a song associate,
something with starlight in it,
blue lilac starlight
and the sound of dipping oars.
I could sing it for them now,
make it up as I go along,
a detailed, useless lyric among shipwrecking green.
In my heart is the surprise of dusk come early
to ancient shapes like tors,
the cold rising vast, these episodes
of silence at last
like eternity.
Sing with me if you want,
or not, my ferryman's song, my siren's song.
Sing for the dead lilacs.

The Gardens Offered in Place of My Mother's Dying

We emptied the books of songs
into rich soil, and all the prophet's names,
in honor of the gardener.

Evenings we studied catalogs and maps,
sketched out parterres, beds, lawns, savannahs, windbreaks,
chose as the guardian stone the flowering fire.

No garden need have walls, but we latticed the perimeters.
We planted broom, mock orange, yew, holly boxwoods—

islands for the ancestors—
grouped them, let some stand alone.

We imported, improvised,
circled our feet with painted pebbles.

When the angle of the sun was right and moisture laden,
the very air exaggerated aerial perspectives,
the light itself a pilgrimage

to all the years we'd been away that blew full and breathed
like wildflowers down the hillsides
brilliant with news, the throngs advancing.

O the whiter the light, the more we planted.
Everything grew then, everything flowered.
We nearly tired of singing inside such mortal clanging,
such festering, bell-ringing green

that we began to dream of miles of rock,
in our sleep scythed valleys or built a house on stilts
and sat above the treeline seeking out some distant plane—

what we saw against the screen of the horizon
likewise in the sky took dominion.
Yes, even sky became a garden.
The clouds banked west like Shiva's mountain.

We stood in the streets clapping our hands,
ran headlong down the sidewalks til such eternal,
insolent crows exploded from the park trees,

rode wingwide the river thermals,
the updrafts between buildings.

Then who could choose once and for all
between God's cities and the cities of Cain,
between Eden and the abundant weeds flowering among the ruins,
seeding themselves for miles

on the ledges of public buildings,
the hospital, effaced by windows,

ours lit all night, ten stories high,
framed and framing mere fragments of the natural.

Someone had painted roses on the fire escapes
across the alley, set bread out for the pigeons.
Someone had dragged a mattress on a roof.

On a square of bright green carpet no bigger than a door
a table waited, plastic flowers in a bottle like a message.

What did they see when they looked at us,
if they looked at all,
who were the chill inside a room in early spring,
or the dream so strange you might believe
that you inherit memory.

We were the boat in the distance
in the gardens on a plate, setting out beyond the blue bridge.

CAROLYN FORCHÉ
(B. 1950)

Elegy

The page opens to snow on a field: boot-holed month, black hour
the bottle in your coat half vodka half winter light.
To what and to whom does one say *yes*?
If God were the uncertain, would you cling to him?

Beneath a tattoo of stars the gate opens, so silent so like a tomb.
This is the city you most loved, an empty stairwell
where the next rain lifts invisibly from the Seine.

With solitude, your coat open, you walk
steadily as if the railings were there and your hands weren't passing
    through them.

"When things were ready, they poured on fuel and touched off the fire.
They waited for a high wind. It was very fine, that powdered bone.
It was put into sacks, and when there were enough we went to a bridge
    on the Narew River."

And even less explicit phrases survived:
"To make charcoal.
For laundry irons."
And so we revolt against silence with a bit of speaking.
The page is a charred field where the dead would have written
We went on. And it was like living through something again one could
    not live through again.

The soul behind you no longer inhabits your life: the unlit house
with its breathless windows and a chimney of ruined wings
where wind becomes an aria, your name, voices from a field,
And you, smoke, dissonance, a psalm, a stairwell.

from The Notebook of an Uprising

[IV]

So we are going back, to the invisible railyard shed and the poppy-seed cakes.
Anna, coal-eyed in a field of bone chips.

When you were born a steamed pot lid was shaken over your face to
provide tears for a lifetime.
       This is why you have such happiness no matter what.
Were these the animals of your village? Pigs, goats, geese, a few cows?

Pigs with their throats cut. Goats eating flowers. Crows descending on
a child to pull hair for their nests.

You loved the shabbiness of the world: countries invaded, cities
bombed, houses whose roofs have fallen in,
       women who have lost their men, orphans, amputees, the war
wounded.
What you did not love any longer was a world that had lost its soul.

[X]

Beyond the tarred Teplice road, past cut fields, tarpaulin-covered
hayricks,
       petrochemical plants spewing black smoke,
Poppies afflicted the hayfields with wounding brilliance.

The people were harvesting cauliflower then from the gardens of
Terezin.
Blank-eyed, a boy pedaled a bicycle back and forth with a naked broken
doll in its basket.

At the prison gate a woman stood holding a bouquet of leeks wrapped
in paper.
Two Czech soldiers strolled through what had once been the women's
compound.
Doors opened and closed, swallows dipped into the prison yard and
rose.
We walked the cold, swept-clean barracks, ran our hands down long
trestle tables and tiered bunks.

We picked forget-me-nots and left them where he died.
Somewhere here, somewhere with his name carved into a wall, are the
  words
      into your sun-blessed life.

[XI]

In the café across from Zivnostenská banka we are able to buy
      a sack of bread for the road, and poppies.
In the tin light we walk, our sandwiches in foil
      like the light along Národní, street of the kiosks.

The wind has eaten the faces from the angels of Charles Bridge
      as if the earth were finished with us.

We leave our *konvalinka* for the saint, white tulips for the mother of
  God.

[XVIII]

We find her in a block of worker housing flats on a small *náměsti*
  bordering a ditch
      near one of the places where
Hitler could have been stopped.

Her name appears in a column of names: *Borovská*.

My voice fills the call box:
"This is the granddaughter of Anna Bassarová and the daughter of
  Michal."

There was so much weeping, she said, but never anyone.
A language even paper would refuse,
bell music rolling down the cold roofs,
their footsteps disappearing as they walked.

She stood on the landing of disbelief in Brno as if the war were
  translucent behind us,
      the little ones in graves the size of pillows.

East Berlin is swept clean, its walks sheltered by oaks. There is nothing
  to buy. People
        stroll and talk, they queue at bookstores.
No one knows where Brecht is buried or where Benjamin lived.

Wie im himmel so auf erden as in heaven so on earth.
Wer ist unser gott? who is our god?

A sign behind the black-windowed Reichstag reads "these are the last
  days."

Breaking holes in the wall, they found nothing.
The homeless squatters passed through the holes into empty
  communist gardens,
        and the people from the east passed from their side
        into a world unbearable to them.

The Garden Shukkei-en

By way of a vanished bridge we cross this river
as a cloud of lifted snow would ascend a mountain.

She has always been afraid to come here.

It is the river she most
remembers, the living
and the dead both crying for help.

A world that allowed neither tears nor lamentation.

The *matsu* trees brush her hair as she passes
beneath them, as do the shining strands of barbed wire.

Where this lake is, there was a lake,
where these black pine grow, there grew black pine.

Where there is no teahouse I see a wooden teahouse
and the corpses of those who slept in it.

On the opposite bank of the Ota, a weeping willow
etches its memory of their faces into the water.

Where light touches the face, the character for heart is written.

She strokes a burnt trunk wrapped in straw:
I was weak and my skin hung from my fingertips like cloth

Do you think for a moment we were human beings to them?

She comes to the stone angel holding paper cranes.
Not an angel, but a woman where she once had been,
who walks through the garden Shukkei-en
calling the carp to the surface by clapping her hands.

Do Americans think of us?

So she began as we squatted over the toilets:
If you want, I'll tell you, but nothing I saw will be enough.

We tried to dress our burns with vegetable oil.

Her hair is the white froth of rice rising up kettlesides, her mind also.
In the postwar years she thought deeply about how to live.

The common greeting *dozo-yiroshku* is please take care of me.
All *hibakusha* still alive were children then.

A cemetery seen from the air is a child's city.

I don't like this particular red flower because
it reminds me of a woman's brain crushed under a roof.

Perhaps my language is too precise, and therefore difficult to
    understand?

We have not, all these years, felt what you call happiness.
But at times, with good fortune, we experience something close.
As our life resembles life, and this garden the garden.
And in the silence surrounding what happened to us

it is the bell to awaken God that we've heard ringing.

JORIE GRAHAM
(B. 1951)

Pietà

—Then the sunshine striking all sides of his body but only
in pieces, in bits—the torso torn from the back, from the arm
that falls back, then three
fingers ripped up by the light into view,

then the lifted knee taken up, taken back, then the ankle, the back of

the head—Like an explosion that will not end
this dismemberment which is her lifting him up, dismemberment
of flesh into minutes. Are they notes, these parts, what is the
song, can you hear it, does it sound beautiful and true to the one

on the other side who hears it all at

once, cadenza of gaps? When she still had him in her,
unseen, unbroken, what did she have?
Before she gets him back there is something he has to cross,
as god, as thief, something he has to marry—Meanwhile

to his left the linen garment he has discarded

is held up by five soldiers
bartering for it, blazing where the light snags on the delicate
embroidery, and black where the neck-hole gapes, black
where the body is seen to be

missing, the form

gone. The five boys bid on it, chance holds it up in the slight wind
and takes their coins for it, this souvenir of the world murmuring
nothing nothing which sounds like God
hast Thou forsaken

me, a small cry fed onto the back of the breeze, small

among the dusksounds, among the opening cries of the early
nightfeeders, small metered cry the breeze takes in among the
    prey cries,
among the price cries. Listen. Do you hear it at
last, the spirit of

matter, there, where the words end—their small heat—where the
    details

cease, the scene dissolves, do you feel it at last, the sinking, where the
                                                                    meaning

rises, where the meaning evaporates, into history, into the day the
mind, and the precipitating syllables are free at last
on the wind, sinking, the proof of god the cry sinking to where it's

just sound, part of one sound, one endless sound—maybe a cry maybe a

countdown, love—

Evening Prayer

Someone has cut the grass. Someone has cut your tall
    new grass, the sweetness
smears a wild raw dress onto the air, and she
is rising, turning now,
                        in sun, in wind, and she

is free. . . . Walking home
I saw the shadow of a bird, like a heart, like a scythe.
I saw the shadow-wings cross through a wall.

The vacant-lot weeds, too, swayed there. And thistles,
    pods. Terrible
silky wall, abandoned warehouse, thigh. . . .
And the elms, burnt now, were young
all over it, and the wind

in its fatigue. . . .
          But the bird, fistful of time and sinew, blue,
dragged down over the cinderblock by light, lawed down and
brushstroked down—how he went through, went
    abstract,
clean. Not hungry there and not afraid. Thou shalt

dash it to pieces, then, Hand-in-the-light, this potter's
    vessel, vast atomic
girl, shall clean it further, further, spill
    the hollow from her, know her?

JOY HARJO
(B. 1951)

Bleed Through

I don't believe in promises, but there you are,
balancing on a tightrope of sound.
                               You sneak into the world
inside a labyrinth of flame
                    break the walls beneath my ribs.
I yearn to sing; a certain note can spiral stars,
               or knock the balance of the world askew.
Inside your horn lives a secret woman
           who says she knows the power of the womb,
can transform massacres into gold, her own heartache
                 into a ruby stone.
Her anger is yours and when her teeth bite through
               a string of glass
you awaken
          and it is not another dream, but your arms
          around a woman
          who was once a dagger between your legs.
There are always ways to fall asleep,
             but to be alive is to forsake
             the fear of blood.
And dreams aren't excuses anymore. You are not behind
             a smoking mirror,
but inside a ceremony of boulders that has survived
             your many deaths.
It is not by accident you watch the sun
            become your heart
      sink into your belly, then reappear in a town
             that magnetically
               attracts you.

What attracts cannot naturally be separated.
　　　　A black hole reversed is a white hot star,
　　　　　　　　　　unravels this night
inside a song that is the same wailing cry as blue.

　　　There are no words, only sounds
　　　　　　　that lead us into the darkest nights,
where stars burn into ice
　　　　　　where the dead arise again
　　　　　　　　　to walk in shoes of fire.

BRENDA HILLMAN
(B. 1951)

First Thought

The first thought
was rage—

In certain systems, the point at which that thought
emerges from God's mind is his consort,
but before she turns her rage onto the world, the violent
lords must give her the body of a woman which is not easy.
Imagine them standing around before they will trap
God's vague thought into female flesh.
The way their robes undulate, the slightly yellowing raiment—

poor things.
They will not understand the rage.
It will be expressed forever in the split in things.
In the two-toned lupine,
in the cupped, silk lining of the tulip,
in the red and white of all armies in all wars,
it will bend over my dream wearing his face.

The moment my daughter was lifted
from me, that sticky
flesh screamed fury,
for she, too, blamed the female body—
I loved it that she screamed—

and I knew I had been sent to earth to understand that pain.

The nurses moved about, doing something
over to the left. Probably weighing her
on what looked like blue tin. The flash of non-
existence always at the edge of vision,
and in the next moment, some unasked-for radiance.

Under those lights,
the nurses seemed shabby—
the ivory lords, come haltingly
into the bridal chamber, slightly yellowing raiment.

The last pain on earth will not be the central pain,
it will be the pain of the soul and not the body,
the pain of the body will be long since gone,
absorbed into the earth, which made it beautiful—

don't you love the word raiment?
Dawn comes in white raiment.
Something like that.

First Tractate

That the soul got to choose. Nothing else
got to but the soul
got to choose.
That it was very clever, stepping
from Lightworld to lightworld
as an egret fishes through its smeared reflections—

through its deaths—
for it believed in the one life,
that it would last forever.

When she had just started being dead I called to her.
Plum trees were waiting to be entered,
the swirling way they have,
each a shower of
What.
Each one full of hope,
and of the repetitions—

When she had been dead a while
I called again. I thought she was superior somehow
because she had become invisible,
because she had become subtle
among the shapes—

and at first she didn't answer; everything answered.

Tell now red-tailed hawk
(for we have heard the smallest thing cry out beneath you):
have you seen her?
(Red hawk) Thrush walking up
the ragged middle:

have you seen her? Mockingbird with your trills
and scallops, with your second mouth
in your throat of all things
tell us:
where is she whom we love?

I closed my eyes and saw the early spring,
pretty spring, kind of a reward;
I opened them and saw the swirling world,
thousands of qualified
pinks, deer feeding
on the torn changes

and I wanted to go back 'from whence' I came.

Up the coast,
along sandbanks and spillways,
the argued-about bays, spring came forth
with its this 'n' that, its I can't
decide, as my life had
before she died: preblossoming:
cranesbill, poppy—

and I wanted to go back "from whence" I came.

Heart that can still see our heart
Heart that will not let us rest

February evening—
young mothers in the drugstore with valentines
all of which needed to be used.
Packages of plain or lace ones
stuck together. And the mothers
proud of themselves for remembering,

the valentines slumped down so the red
merely looked promising
but pressing up bravely anyhow—

the awkwardness of what's here,
ceaselessly trying to arrange itself;

I went out in the night, I called out,
I felt along the edges of the panel:
without her,
everything seemed strange to me in this world;
just the taste of oranges: imagine!

And all of this compared to her seemed bulky.
For weeks this was true.
As if only being dead were the right amount.
Only being dead were fragile enough
for what the earth had to say.
Clumsy. For a while. Clumsy. For a while
it was too much to go on living.
Roadside acacias—
I could not bear them. All unzipped,
like meaning.
The ostinatos of the birds.
Magnolias—dogs'-tongues—curved
to spoon up rain. Too much shape.
Even that which was only suspected
of having it: the iris
that lay in the ground with their eyes of fate.

And then the other voice said

You who long for things
who can't understand borders
who like to spread your magic and your blame
forgive yourself.

She'd given you an impossible task:

she said to follow and you intended to.
But you'd come to a place in the forest
where there weren't any tracks—

SHU DING (SHU TING)
(B. 1952)

Two or Three Incidents Recollected

An overturned cup of wine.
A stone path sailing in moonlight.
Where the blue grass is flattened,
an azalea flower abandoned.

The eucalyptus wood swirls.
Stars above teem into a kaleidoscope.
On a rusty anchor,
eyes mirror the dizzy sky.

Holding up a book to shade the candle
and with a finger in between the lips,
I sit in an eggshell quiet,
having a semi-transparent dream.

(*translated by Tony Barnstone and Chou Ping*)

ANITA ENDREZZE
(B. 1952)

November Harvest

Barns huddle over the horns
of cattle, whose dreams
are four-chambered,
the white hearts of winter.

In the shadows of thorns,
the farmers are without
substance.
Under the roots,
the warm slow sleepers
are not dreaming of us.
Their breaths pass into
the myths of animals.

All November fields are dark
passages into the earth.
What the owl flies into
we call night.
The moon is a windfall, a pear
weathering to the core.
The scarecrow is quiet;
a small wind lifts
his eyeless sack of a head.
When the Harvest God comes,
he wears a suit black
as parson's cloth.
His tongue is a brown leaf,
his sermon a mouthful of wheat.
What we leave in the fields
is his: misshapen pumpkins,
spotted apples, rotted beans.

Where the soft decay touches
the soil, mouths form,
then heads thick as clay,
bodies like corn shocks,
hands, fingers, legs, toes
like odd-sized gourds.

In the furrows of our beds,
we hear their clumping walk
and dream of weak breaths,
lungfuls of seeds.
They circle our houses,
tapping the windows,
their pale tongues
sprouting out to us
in our mutual darkness.

AMINA SAÏD
(B. 1953)

The Bird Is Mediation

the bird is mediation
by virtue of wing
and song

and that palpitation
which gives it life

and that language too
a quest in the clear
silence of the night

if it travel down a road
of fire
between earth sea and sky
is it not reborn
aloft
from its trail of ashes?

like a soul which awakes
to the unknown
it will come from the tattered
heart of a cloud
to alight on the tree of the world

On the Tattered Edges . . .

on the tattered edges of my unravelling memory
heiress of time
the water and sand sing in my veins

before my eyes springs
abundance ringed round by the barest deserts
of your horizonless freedom your prison without bars

you rediscover a destiny
in the figurines born of hard night
many strange things indeed
to search through until a name comes to mind

the madman and his monster
as though they were dying furiously digging
their own graves in the depths of violent sleep

and in the sands of memory
only the tracks of two bodies
and no one notices
the cold enemy
returning calmly
to prowl with the stark morning

they are only whispers
I shall go out under the sun
to sing with the loudest voice

My Woman's Transparence

my woman's transparence
has the whole sea
as its mirror

my sea-spray is born
of the salt of its peaks

my voice plays echo
to its thunder
and to its murmurs

we   were
as one sea-swell
when   we strode
toward land

we   joined hands

(*translated by Eric Sellin*)

RACHIDA MADANI
(B. 1953)

Here I Am Once More . . .

Here I am once more before the sea
smashing whole doors against the rocks
mingling in the same bitter rolling motion
sand and pearls
in the burning metallic waves
the jasmine of my childhood and the shriek-owl of hell.

Here I am once more before the sea, bent over
under the annual booty of rancour
of fatigue
and of cocks slaughtered throats cut to no avail
for the well-being of a turban
which for a long time now has been
no more than a heap of dust
smirking under a slab
while in the shade of a fig tree
women and candles burn
to do magic with the eye
bad luck
and the raven of despair.

For an amulet did I too
swap my gold tooth
and the henna on my hands
and unclasp my eyes,
did I too look at the moon
and drink bowls
of the liquid verb, still and black?
I also kept staring
at the boats and the storks which were leaving
but we women all waited
                    in vain

in tears
for our fathers, loved ones
sons and brothers.

But the city opens wide the jaws
of its prisons
swallows them with its tea
and then fans itself.
But the city pulls its knives
whittles us a body without limbs
a face without a voice
but the city bears its heart
as we do our walls,
but the city . . .
I hurt even down to my shadow cast
upon the other sidewalk
where my latest poems are strewn
in little crystals of opaque salts
like icy tears.
My head falls down on my chest
like a mortar shell
seen from close up, my heart is a lake.

(*translated by Eric Sellin*)

ROSANNA WARREN
(B. 1954)

Max Jacob at Saint Benoît

The noonday square. Plane leaves, dust:
they scurry in heat shimmering gusts.
Even shadows rustle. The Belgians are gone.
The tiny terrier trots alone.
Max prayed here, *le grand poseur,*
salon mystic and *littérateur,*
but fourteen years, remember, that's one hell
of a pose for a Paris swell.
He had an infallible sense of scene.
See that stone soul torn limb from limb
between the devils and seraphim?
Romanesque, of course, for Max to preen
his own soul's pretty plumage here
year after tiresome dusty year.
And still, it wasn't easy. *Quel ennui!*
This flat, hot land, the sluggish Loire;
daily, nightly, daily: *prière, devoir;*
no more blue-yellow visions of Christ on the tree
(from Max's aquarelle), no more *cinémathèque*
blue movie Maries scolding *"pauvre Max"*
(to scandalize confessors),
no more dandified mystics dogging his tracks.
At Saint Benoît, just dust. The trek
to God? Beyond the crypt, it led
from boredom to boredom to prison camp bed
in Drancy. There, the Nazis let him die
—an old Jew with pneumonia—"naturally."

LOUISE ERDRICH
(B. 1955)

Fooling God

I must become small and hide where he cannot reach.
I must become dull and heavy as an iron pot.
I must be tireless as rust and bold as roots
growing through the locks on doors
and crumbling the cinderblocks
of the foundations of his everlasting throne.
I must be strange as pity so he'll believe me.
I must be terrible and brush my hair
so that he finds me attractive.
Perhaps if I invoke Clare, the patron saint of television.
Perhaps if I become the images
passing through the cells of a woman's brain.

I must become very large and block his sight.
I must be sharp and impetuous as knives.
I must insert myself into the bark of his apple trees,
and cleave the bones of his cows. I must be the marrow
that he drinks into his cloud-wet body.
I must be careful and laugh when he laughs.
I must turn down the covers and guide him in.
I must fashion his children out of playdough, blue, pink, green.
I must pull them from between my legs
and set them before the television.

I must hide my memory in a mustard grain
so that he'll search for it over time until time is gone.
I must lose myself in the world's regard and disparagement.
I must remain this person and be no trouble.
None at all. So he'll forget.
I'll collect dust out of reach,
a single dish from a set, a flower made of felt,
a tablet the wrong shape to choke on.

I must become essential and file everything
under my own system,
so we can lose him and his proofs and adherents.
I must be a doubter in a city of belief
that hails his signs (the great footprints
long as limousines, the rough print on the wall).
On the pavement where his house begins
fainting women kneel. I'm not among them
although they polish the brass tongues of his lions
with their own tongues
and taste the everlasting life.

ALIKI BARNSTONE
(B. 1956)

Blue

Blue is Greece where fishermen tame their boats,
where I float naked in the color of truth, the sea

humming in my ears, lulling me with ultramarines
like a baby kicking in amniotic seas, like god

whose throne is this transparent blue bowl,
this star-sapphire studded cradle of waves.

She must have blue skin and eyes, lapis lazuli
looped in strands and strands around her rounded belly

and her breasts amply squirting blue-white milk.
She must make love on silk sheets of azure air.

She must have been there in the window,
that narrow shaft in the hospital wall letting in

pale blue spring light the morning my daughter was born.
She hid in the forget-me-nots in the wallpaper,

fluttered in the doctors' and nurses' blue medical gowns,
glinted in the metallic blue of the scissors that cut the cord.

Her blue threads embroidered the bloody placenta.
She colors the newborns' eyes blue

for babies come from her inside-out world.
She is in the bluish spit against the evil eye.

When I'm blue I close my eyes and see blue with my third eye.
Blue light comes from the island in my brain

where sunflowers crook their necks, weary of time.
Sunflowers, your wild fire hair burns in blue.

Peaceful blue, luminous blue, keep my daughter safe.
She splashes her little feet in Aegean blue sea,

reaches her hands into blue beauty. I hug her dry
in a towel deep blue as Mary's timeless robes.

Bathing Jesus

If he were a word made flesh I would want to wake him from his
   godliness
and wash his godliness from him as I bathe his feet in my laughing tears
and dry them with my heat and hair and anoint the topography
   of his head with euphoric oil
and comb his beard with electric fingers and pull his face close to mine
to see the multitudes in the pores in his skin, God's intricate human
   handiwork in his cheek.
He would see the flame in my eye burning in time's skull, deep
   as the first breath that lighted the Milky Way.
I would pull the shirt from his shoulders and the shirt from mine
until our garments lay on the floor, cloth lungs pulsating
   with the curtain's white muslin and the little breezes
   coming in the window, everything alive,
even the wood floor under our feet warm with the oak's broad
   and branching spirit.
And I would pour warm water on his back and thighs and wake
   the man in him, wake his hand
reaching for my flushed and water-slicked arm, his palm singeing
   the place below my collarbone,
make him taste each word on my tongue, each complex mix of sweet
   and bitter and sour and salt
and make him sing out from his body, *the lips, the tongue, the throat,*
   the heart, the blood, all the traveling heats of flesh. Praise them.
I would stand before him naked as Eve before the Fall
   or a babe newborn
and he would see no sin on my skin, if he were a word made flesh.

LUCIE BROCK-BROIDO
(B. 1956)

Of the Finished World

Open the final book: November spills
Its lamplit light, the clenched astronomer hunched

At table, considering his vexed celestial
Map, illegible as the flinch

Of needles falling on the blanched
Rye fields in pentagrams.

The harvest is done with itself, its ransack
Done. The wild coated horses bunch

In the clot of darkness that falls on the land.
In the thrice-ploughed field, picked

Clean, what is left of the bottle-gourds
Will freeze by night, a ruined hour

From here. On the freighted road, laden with
Old hunger & apocrypha, a heaven sloughs

Its midden things, things left of the unfinished
World, its most hideous & permanent

Impermanence. As long as I am, I am
Hither—here—a little mob of Spoon

& Ladle, Sugar-Trough, a clinched antinomy
Of will. I was not awake for any war to speak

Of. Suddenly I cannot see any more in the dark
Where the grains amass in their silo stacks.

In the finished world, I will be wind-awry,
Will be out of mind, in asylum

Of the quiet that fell on a clotted room
Where even the astronomer can no longer

Attend to the tenebrous world undone.
How have I lived here so long?

The One Thousand Days

There is the mourning dish of salt outside
My door, a cup of quarantine, saucerless, a sign

That one inside had been taken down
By grieving, ill tongue-tied will or simple

Illness, yet trouble came.
I have found electricity in mere ambition,

If nothing else, yet to make myself sick on it.
A spectacle of marvelling & discontent

Let me tell you how it came to this.
I was turning over the tincture of things,

I was trying to recollect the great maroon
Portière of everything that had ever happened,

When the light first stopped its transport
& the weather ceased to be interesting,

Then the dark drape closed over the altar
& a minor city's temple burnt to ground.

I was looking to become inscrutable.
I was longing to be seen through.

It was at slaughtering, it
Was at the early stain

Of autumn when the dirt-
Tinted lambs were brought down

From the high unkempt fields of Sligo, bidden,
Unbidden, they came down.

It was then that I was quit
Of speech, a thousand northbound nights of it.

Then was ambition come
Gleaming up like a fractured bone.

As it breaks through the bodiced veil of skin.
I marry into it, a thistle on

The palm, salt-pelt on
The slaughtering, & trouble came.

That the name of bliss is only in
The diminishing—as far as possible—of pain.

That I had quit the quiet velvet cult of it,
Yet trouble came.

Physicism

In the valley of the Euphrates, each
Of the stars had certain shepherds

To the people there. Here, in this small valley
Showered with emboli, we each have none.

Before the Babylonians, the sun was called
Old Sheep, the planets Old Sheep Stars.

Under the blood sky here, in the physicism
Of waiting for my dusk, nothing is lunular

Yet. Animal, mineral, domajigger, clock.
There are blood-sheep everywhere,

But no shepherds left. Only blood sisters here,
All with the color taken from sight.

They live in black & white, material
& motherless beneath the widgit-slang of sky.

Phenomenal on the long aortic pulse
Of equinox, a Sumerian describes his stars

Collectively as *flock* & it is heavenly to him.
Here there is no heaven here.

Unforgettable, for All My Uncertainty
as to What It Is I Am Remembering

The reason why I love the orchard is my propensity for lavish
Order in certain seasons of the year, a Glaswegian

Gloom ascends as snow apples fall long before the snow is
Come. When she died, it may as well have spooned the quince-

Shaped heart from me. Forgiveness, in this agnostic time, was
Not a possibility, the way each pome fruit orchard was

A whole tin bucket of despairs, singly as benign as
Silvernerve, in accumulation something powerful & poisonous.

A hearse moves through the city like a herd of
One, bison-like & woolly in the summer sun, carnivorous.

Recall the kitchen & your half-learned love, the room you know
She will never be inside again, & someone telling you:

She is not here, she is not anywhere, you see, & you were there;
It was the last time you would be at home, in harm.

Soul Keeping Company

The hours between washing & the well
Of burial are the soul's most troubled time.

I sat with her in keeping company
All through the afflict of the night, keeping

Soul constant, a second self. Earth is heavy
& I made no wish, save being

Merely magical. I am magical
No more. This, I well remember well.

In the sweet thereafter the impress
Of the senses will be tattooed to

The whole world ravelling in the clemency
Of an autumn of Octobers, all that bounty

Bountiful & the oaks specifically
Afire as everything dies off, inclining

To the merciful. I would have made of my body
A body to protect her, anything to keep

Her well & here—in the soul's suite
Before five tons of earth will bear

On her, stay here
Soul, in the good night of my company.

NOTES ON THE POETS

ENHEDUANNA (born ca. 2300 BCE)   A moon priestess and daughter of the Sumerian king Sargon of Kkad (2334–2279 BCE), Enheduanna is the first recorded poet in the world. Her work was preserved on cuneiform tablets. In her poems to the Sumerian Goddess of love, Inanna (also known as Ishtar), she speaks to a deity who has descended to earth as an ally, as a friend to help her in need. The poems' sensuality, surprising metaphors, and intimacy anticipate Sappho's poems to her ally Aphrodite. Yet unlike Sappho, Enheduanna speaks with the rhetorical grandeur of the biblical Hebrew prophets when she evokes the cosmic forces of nature and the gods.

QUEEN HATSHEPSUT (d. 1482 BCE)   The pharaoh queen of Egypt of the eighteenth dynasty, Hatshepsut ruled from ca. 1503 to 1482 BCE. The daughter of Thutmose I, she relegated her husband Thutmose II to the background, and of the five pharaoh queens she was by far the most significant. During her peaceful reign she developed resources in Egypt and built the famous temple of Deir el-Bahri near Thebes and also erected five gigantic obelisks in the temple of Amun Re at Karnak. Her poem is a strong apologia for her reign. Hatshepsut referred to herself in her poem as both male and female, son and daughter, and claimed that the sun god Amun Re was her father.

ANONYMOUS EGYPTIAN (ca. 1500 BCE)   Ezra Pound and Noel Stock have given us pristine versions of ancient Egyptian love poems, which appear remarkably personal, intimate, and modern. Love is the most refined spiritual art in Egyptian writing. Women's poetry of the Middle East has a principal source in Egypt. Scholars also propose that the biblical Song of Songs has its origin in Egyptian love songs, with which it has a remarkable affinity.

ANONYMOUS JEW (10th–3rd centuries BCE)   The Song of Songs is a collection of love songs, which in its present form appears to be a fragmentary love idyll, with a dramatic structure. The sole book of love poems in the Bible, the work was attributed to Solomon, as the Psalms (also *shir*, meaning "song" in Hebrew) were attributed to David in order to be accepted into the holy canon. However, the actual authorship of the Song of Songs is unknown and is of a much later date than Solomon. It has two voices, female and male. The excerpts included here are in the woman's voice.

SAPPHO (b. 630–612 BCE) Born on the island of Lesbos (from which *lesbian* derives), Sappho was married and had a daughter, Kleis, to whom she wrote poems. Other love poems were written to her woman followers. "Some say nine Muses—but count again," Plato wrote. "Behold the tenth: Sappho of Lesbos." During the early Christian period her poems, in abundant copies, were destroyed by order of the pope due to religious hostility toward her erotic and religious poems. Although we have only one complete poem, the prayer or ode to Aphrodite found in Longinus's essay *On the Sublime,* many small and large fragments remain, enough to give us a full picture of the poet's work. Sappho is a major poet of Greek and Roman antiquity.

ZI YE (Tzu Yeh) (6th–3rd centuries BCE?) These anonymous popular songs in the *zi* form were originally attributed to a woman poet of that name, but this notion is now rejected, since they appear to be written by many authors over a period of three hundred years. The collection remains a major source of the tradition of short songs of extraordinary art, pathos, and subtle spirit. Some 123 Zi Ye songs have been preserved.

PATACARA (6th–5th centuries BCE?) Patacara was a banker's daughter in northern India. When her children, husband, and parents were suddenly killed by natural disasters, she went mad and wandered naked in circles in the forest till the Buddha found her. He threw a robe on her and told her, "In your many lives, you have shed more tears for the dead than there is water in the four oceans." With these words she attained enlightenment.

SANGHA (6th–5th centuries BCE?) Although said to have been a member of Prince Siddhartha Gautama's large harem, her poem suggests that she was a keeper of cows and a member of the *vaishya* caste. Her work is in Pali in the *Therigatha,* the book of enlightenment poetry of Buddhist nuns.

SAKULA (6th–5th centuries BCE?) Sakula was of the Brahman caste. When she chose to become a nun, Gautama (the Buddha) chose her as foremost of nuns, possessing the psychic power of the "eye of heaven," meaning that she could see into all worlds, near and far.

DANTIKA (6th–5th centuries BCE?)   A daughter of a minister of an Indian kingdom, Dantika went to the forest for solitude and subsisted on fruits and roots. As one of the earliest followers of Siddhartha Gautama (the Buddha), she was a wandering ascetic nun, a renunciant (*samana*), who gave up privilege, as did Siddhartha, to attain nirvana.

NANDUTTA (6th–3rd centuries BCE?)   From a brahman family in northeast India, Nandutta lived in the kingdom of Jurus. She became famous and traveled around India with a rose-apple branch in her hand, debating religion with challengers. In one debate with a Buddhist, she met her match, converted to Buddhism and found a new freedom.

ANONYMOUS BUDDHIST SISTER (6th–3rd centuries BCE?)   The nun records the basic principles that caused her to convert to Buddhism.

SISUPACALA (6th–3rd centuries BCE?)   One of four children of a brahman, Sisupacala converted to Buddhism and wrote poems. Like her sister nuns, she wrote, or her songs were recorded, in Pali, a northern version of Sanskrit.

SUMANGALA'S MOTHER (6th–3rd centuries BCE?)   Her poem "I Am a Free Woman" survives in Pali as an example of a woman freed, through action and Buddhist meditation, of the burden of a cruel husband. The author is said to have been a weaver of straw hats.

GOVINDASVAMIN (5th century BCE–1000 CE?)   Nothing is known about this poet but her name. See "Anonymous Sanskrit Songs."

ANONYMOUS SANSKRIT SONGS (5th century BCE–1000 CE?)   These anonymous classical Sanskrit songs have traditionally been attributed to diverse poets, without certainty. Erotic and divine love intertwine in India, as in many traditions—Jewish (Song of Songs), Christian (Donne, John of the Cross), and Muslim (Sufi mystics). In Sanskrit poetry, which lives off love, the sexual poetry is religious, and sometimes, to fool the husband or reader, the Lord is evoked to excuse the erotic.

PRAXILLA (ca. 450 BCE)   Only a few fragments of her beautiful poems are extant, though Praxilla from the Argolid wrote abundantly and in diverse meters. She has the honor of having her lines preserved because hostile critics cited them to show the "nonsense" in her poetry. So Zenobios fumed "only a simpleton would put cucumbers and the like on a par with the sun and the moon."

KORINNA (late 3rd century BCE)   A Boiotian poet, Korinna wrote narrative choral lyrics for an audience of women. Aelianus wrote of her, "When Pindar the poet competed at Thebes he ran into ignorant judges, and was defeated five times by Korinna. To show the judges' bad taste, Pindar called Korinna a pig." Plutarch wrote in praise of Korinna, "When Pindar was still young and proud of his mastery of the language, Korinna censured him for his poor taste."

MIRYAM, MOTHER OF YESHUA (Mary, Mother of Jesus) (1st century CE)   "The Magnificat" is the Latin title found in the Vulgate Bible, which is the Latin translation of the Greek New Testament. Miryam speaks this canticle in Luke 1:46–55. The poem exists in Greek, and like the songs of Deborah and Hannah, the song of Miryam is in the tradition of parallelistic Hebrew poetry.

ANONYMOUS INDIAN (1st century CE)   Found in Prakrita (a dialect of Sanskrit) and in Sanskrit translation, the collection for King Hala of more than seven hundred *gathas* contains every mood of spiritual and sexual love.

ANONYMOUS GNOSTIC REVEALER (2nd–3rd centuries CE)   "The Thunder, Perfect Mind" is a revelation discourse by a female revealer in the first person. The religious tradition of the poet is difficult to classify as Jewish, Christian, Gnostic, or combinations of these traditions. As the translator, George McRae, states, it proclaims "the absolute transcendence of the revealer, whose greatness is incomprehensible and whose being is unfathomable." The text, in Coptic translation from the Greek, is part of the Gnostic Nag Hammadi Papyri uncovered in Egypt in 1945.

AL-KHANSA (575–646 CE)   Born in Mecca or Medina, Arabia, al-Khansa was a member of a powerful family, some of whom were poets. Almost all her poems deal with the death of her two brothers, Sakhr and Muawiya, whom she laments with Homeric, epical strength. They were killed in a tribal battle before Islam came to Arabia. Addressing poems to one's brother was a necessary allegory for writing poems to one's lover, or even to a godhead. Al-Khansa is a fiercely strong poet, earthy, wildly imaginative, using desert and tribal details to produce shocking, poignant images which only in the twentieth century have poets ventured to use. She is one of the major poets in Arabic and considered by many the outstanding poet of classical Arabic.

RABIA THE MYSTIC (712–801)   Rabia was born in Basra, in present-day Iraq. As a child of a poor family, she was captured and sold into slavery until, apparently because of a spiritual light that shone around her like a lamp, she was freed. Later she turned down good marriage offers for the life of an ascetic. Though she was a Sufi mystic in the Persian tradition, there are also strong Gnostic and Plotinian echoes in her work. Because of miracles with her name, she is a Muslim saint.

YESHE TSOGYEL (757?–817?)   Yeshe Tsogyel lived during the heroic period of Tibetan history when the military power was prominent and feared throughout central Asia. She is said to have been a princess. Although wed at twelve to a king, she soon went off with a Buddhist master and in the mountains practiced meditation for three years. Later she found her consort in Nepal and on return to Tibet helped establish Buddhism as the state religion.

KASSIA (ca. 840)   Born in Constantinople, Kassia became a nun and wrote words and music for at least twenty-three hymns that are part of Byzantine liturgy. Her "Mary Magdalene" is chanted during Holy Week in the Eastern Orthodox Church, and even today Greeks know her hymns by heart as Western Christians know the carols.

WU CAILUAN (WU TS'AILUAN) (9th century)   According to Taoist legend, Wu Cailuan was the daughter of Wu Meng, a Taoist expert. She studied at a center for feminine alchemy, where she attained the Way. Secular sources say she lived in the ninth century (religious tradition places her in the third and fourth centuries) and was banished to the ordinary world, where she married an impoverished scholar. She earned her living by writing about poetry. Eventually she and her husband disappeared into the mountains.

YU XUANJI (Yü Hsüan-chi) (843–868)   Born in Changan (Ch'ang-an), the capital of Tang China, in her short life Yu Xuanji was a cultivated literary courtesan, a concubine, a Taoist nun, and finally "a criminal" executed on trumped-up charges. When her lover freed her from a brothel and then abandoned her, she became a Taoist nun. She is one of the great Tang nature and metaphysical poets.

ISE SHIKIBU (Lady Ise) (9th–10th centuries)   Daughter of the governor of the province Ise and Yamato, Ise Shikibu spent most of her life in the court of the Emperor Uda and was one of his favorite consorts. She bore him a son, who died at age seven. She also bore a daughter by

Uda's fourth son, Prince Atsuyoshi. She was a lady in waiting for Empress Onshi. Her poems appear in the *Kokinshu*, the first imperial anthology, completed in 905. During her lifetime she was given the epithet, "One of the thirty-six poetic geniuses of Japan."

IZUMI SHIKIBU (Lady Izumi) (974–1034) Izumi Shikibu was the daughter of Oe no Masamune and the wife of Tachibana no Michisada, the lord of Izumi. She was a contemporary of Lady Murasaki, who wrote *The Tale of Genji*, the first great Japanese novel. Izumi Shikibu had many lovers and was the mistress of Prince Tametaka as well as his brother Prince Atsumichi, who was her great love and who died at age twenty-seven. She mourns Prince Atsumichi in more than one hundred poems. Her masterpiece in prose is her diary consisting of correspondence. In this epistolary diary were poems by Izumi Shikibu to and from her lover.

ANONYMOUS JAPANESE TANKA (10th century?) This anonymous tanka has resonances in classical Chinese poems, where the note of a temple bell not only marks a specific time but also symbolizes time in general.

ANONYMOUS LATIN SONG (ca. 1000) From the *Cambridge Songs*, this planctus (lament) is the best-known surviving woman's lament from the Latin Middle Ages.

LI QINGZHAO (Li Ch'ing-chao) (1084–ca. 1151) One of the most famous poets in China, Li Qingzhao was born into a literary family and married Zhao Mingqeng, a man of letters, who like herself was an antiquarian, book collector, and calligrapher. They were an ideal literary couple and assembled a large collection of paintings, seals, bronzes, and manuscripts. When the Qin Tartars invaded Song-dynasty China, they were forced to flee their home. Most of their collection in ten buildings was destroyed. Two years later Li's husband died. Thereafter, she retrieved what she could of their collection and continued to write poems, now not of early happiness but of loss, loneliness, and a spiritual change. Although Li was a prolific writer of some six volumes of lyrics, only seventy-eight songs (*zi*) have survived. Always in control of her poems, Li Qingzhao has the emotional authority of exact observation in which she uses nature and the things of her bedroom as the mirror of her being and spirit. Her *Discourse on the Lyric* is one of the earliest treatments of prosody and poetic theory.

HILDEGARD OF BINGEN (1098–1179) Hildegard of Bingen was born into an aristocratic German family. As a child she had visions that were deemed mystical and prophetic. She entered a religious order of holy women in 1106 at the age of eight. She became abbess of the monastery of Diessenberg twenty years later. In the 1140s she moved her convent to Rupertsberg, near Bingen. After a committee authenticated her visions, she continued her visionary life, dictating her revelations to her brother. Her book *Scivias* contains twenty-six visions. Unlike Saint John of the Cross and other mystics who saw human erotic love in the biblical Song of Songs as the unique human simile to speak of an ineffable divine union with God, Hildegard abhorred the body, which she held to be a vehicle for fornication, and considered pleasures of the flesh to be fiendish inventions of the devil. Her way was resurrection in the light of God's gaze. Although she was not formally canonized, her followers proclaimed her a saint.

SUN BUER (Sun Pu-erh) (1124–?) Sun Buer lived in northern China and was a disciple of Wang Zhe, a founder of the Pure Serenity School of Complete Reality Taoism. Her husband Ma Danyang was also a student of Taoist illuminism. Sun Buer wrote a famous set of fourteen poems and also secret texts. The secret texts describe meditation methods and healing associated with the Taoist science of essence and science of life, the first concerned with spiritual transcendence, the second with temporal health and energy.

ANONYMOUS PROVENÇAL (12th century) In this anonymous poem Domna (Lady) Carenza hears requests from two sisters, Iselda and Alais, about virginity and marriage. They receive a wildly satiric response from Domna Carenza, who suggests they save their maidenhood for God, who has "the best seed from a cod," and who will give them glorious children.

MAHADEVI (12th century) Born in Udutadi, India, Mahadevi at the age of ten was initiated into the worship of Shiva, whom she refers to as the "lord white as jasmine," an epithet that appears in her poems, which she wrote in Kannada. She was forced into an arranged marriage with a local king, but she left him for Shiva and led the life of a poet-saint. She threw away her clothing in a gesture of social defiance and wandered god-intoxicated, covered only by her tresses. According to legend she died into oneness with Shiva when she was still in her twenties, in a brief bright burning.

ZHU XUZHEN (Chu Shu-chen) (ca. 1200) Although many of Zhu Xuzhen's poems survive and her reputation is second only to Li Qingzhao's, virtually nothing is known about her life except what can be derived from her poems. Apparently her parents burned her poems after her death, but copies were preserved by friends. She wrote in the *shi* and *zi* forms and was fully aware of herself as poet: "I write poems, change and correct them, and finally throw them away," she observed.

ANONYMOUS FRENCH SONG (12th–13th centuries) This motet, with humor, anger, and poignancy, shows the erotic plight of a young girl forced into a convent.

BEATRICE OF NAZARETH (ca. 1200–1268) Beatrice of Nazareth was a Beguine visionary (see Hadewijch of Brabant) and the author of an autobiography excerpted here, *Seven Manners of Loving*.

MECHTHILD OF MAGDEBURG (ca. 1212–1282) A Free Spirit Beguine (see Hadewijch of Brabant) given to good works and spiritual love, and a mystico-erotic poet, Mechthild eventually entered a convent.

MUKTABAI (13th century) There are legendary statements about the philosophical and religious poems of Mukta Bai. She and her brothers and sisters survived abandonment by begging. Though her reputation is high, little else is known about her.

HADEWIJCH OF BRABANT (13th century) The greatest name in medieval Flemish/Dutch literature is Hadewijch of Antwerp, or of Brabant (the province), from what is today Belgium. She was probably head of a *béguinage* of the Beguine sect which thrived from the twelfth to the fourteenth centuries in Belgium, Holland, France, and Germany. The women, called Free Spirit nuns, did not take vows, often lived in cottages, and lived a spiritual and charitable life, and many were writers whose work was socially aware and mystical.

WANG QINGHUI (Wang Ch'ing-hui) (13th century) Wang Qinghui's prayer poem of a captured young woman is part of a tradition of poems written by captive women. The reference to the army, "war drums on horseback," is the conquering Mongol army of Kublai Khan, which had captured Hangzhou, the capital of southern Song-dynasty China. Ch'ang-O is the moon goddess.

MARGUERITE PORETE (d. 1310) A member of a free community of the Beguines (see Hadewijch of Brabant), Marguerite Porete wrote prose, poetry, and dialogues in *Mirror of Simple Souls* (1285–1295), a popular book in which she spoke of love and also attacked the established clergy.

Her work was condemned in her native city of Valenciennes around 1300. She was publicly burned. Although her book was also burned, it did not disappear, since copies existed in English, Italian, and Latin translation as well as in French.

SAINT CATHERINE OF SIENA (1347–1380)   An Italian mystic and visionary of the Dominican order, Catherine had visions and practiced austerities from childhood. She was a diplomat who worked with popes and urged a crusade against the Muslims. She is said to have received the five wounds of the stigmata, visible only after death. Although she was illiterate, she dictated hundreds of letters and *A Treatise on Divine Providence,* later called *The Dialogue of Saint Catherine of Siena.*

LAL DED (Lalla) (14th century?)   Lal Ded was born in Kashmir. Married as a child, she was maltreated and neglected. She left her husband to become devoted to Shiva. Like Mahadevi, she wandered naked, danced, and gave herself to mystical union with God.

SISTER BERTKEN (1427?–1514)   Sister Bertken was a medieval Dutch nun about whom little is known, but we do know that she spent fifty-seven years of her life in a Utrecht convent. Her allegorical poems borrow from the Song of Songs.

ANONYMOUS NAHUATL (15th century)   In the early sixteenth century, Spanish missionary friars and priests destroyed all the codices of ancient literature they could find and succeeded in erasing most of the written records of major Maya and Nahuatl (Aztec) pre-Columbian civilizations. However, at the same time, others recorded oral poetry around 1559. The Franciscan friar Bernardino de Sahagun recorded the hymns included here just north of Tenochtitlan (Mexico City), attaching them to the Florentine Codex. But he left them untranslated for fear of their demonic power.

VITTORIA DA COLONNA (1492–1547)   Vittoria da Colonna, also known as marchesa di Pescara, was a celebrated woman of the Italian Renaissance, a friend of poets and artists, including her closest confident, Michelangelo. After her husband's death in 1525 she wrote many poems of grief, and she lived largely in convents, devoting herself to religious reform and writing poems with religious themes. Her poems use a prevalent Neoplatonic Petrarchan imagery, such as "sun" to represent her lover husband.

HUANG E (Huang O) (1498–1569)   Daughter of an official, wife of the poet and dramatist Yang Shen, Huang E wrote erotic poetry—surprising in her time for one not a courtesan, though hers was a permissive age of great erotic novels.

MIRABAI (ca. 1498–1573)   Mirabai is the best-known poet in India and the most-read Indian poet in foreign translation. Her poems are in Hindi but appear from an early period in translation in other Indian languages. Mirabai was probably born in Merta and raised by her grandfather. She was married at eighteen to the Prince of Mewar. She was a rebel in thought, religion, and poetry, and after her husband's death, the local king tried to poison her. She fled and lived in places sacred to Krishna, the god whom her poems address, and died in Dwarka. She was at once humorous, erotic, and ecstatic. Her "dancing" before God, like the whirling of the dervishes, the quaking of Quakers, and the babbling of Spanish mystics, shows a physical detachment from the ordinary as she passes into transcendent elation.

ANONYMOUS SPANISH SONGS (15th–16th centuries)   The General Songbook (Cancionero general), collected by Hernando del Castillo in 1512, contains popular as well as learned poems (poemas cultos), including ballads and songs in traditional Spanish as opposed to "European" French and Italian prosody. The influence of the popular song has always been paramount in Spain, as seen in the baroque poems of Luis de Góngora and in twentieth-century poets Antonio Machado and Federico García Lorca.

LOUISE LABÉ (1525–1566)   Labé was born in Lyons, France, a cultural center where she had a literary salon. She was an accomplished horsewoman and archer and was said to have fought in battle in the ranks of Henry II in his Spanish expedition. Though married to a rope maker, she fell in love with several suitors. When she broke with her second lover, she retired to the country and died a few years later. She wrote initially in Italian, imitating Petrarch.

EMILIA LANIER (1569–1645)   Emilia Bassano was the illegitimate daughter of Baptista Bassano, musician to the queen, and Margaret Johnson. In his book The Poems of Shakespeare's Dark Lady, A. L. Rowse claims that Sonnets 127 through 152, those to the so-called Dark Lady, were addressed to Emilia Lanier, who was then married to Alphonso Lanier. Her long work, Salve Deus Rex Judeorum (1611), is a skilled work of historical and biblical events in which she argues for the virtue of Eve, Deborah, Judith, Esther, Susanna, and Cleopatra. Independent of any possible connection with Shakespeare, she is an outstanding poet of her age, the English counterpart to Anne Bradstreet for both her artistry and her passion for clarifying the plight and virtues of women.

SOR VIOLANTE DO CÉU (1602?–1693)   Born in Lisbon, Violante Montesino entered the Our Lady of the Rosary order in 1630. A well-known poet who wrote in Portuguese in the manner of the Spanish golden age poets Luis de Góngora and Francisco de Quevedo, her play *Saint Eufemia* was performed before Phillip III of Spain.

ANNE BRADSTREET (1612?–1672)   Bradstreet was born in Northamptonshire, England, and arrived as a Puritan Pilgrim in the colony of Massachusetts on the ship *Arabella* in 1630. Her husband, Simon Bradstreet, was to become governor of the colony. Bradstreet's poems combine personal detail and events—the births and deaths of her children, illnesses, her husband, the burning of her house—and are replete with Puritan allegory, mythological allusions, and metaphysical conceits reminiscent of her compatriot Edward Taylor and the longer poems of John Donne. Her role as the first American poet is the basis for John Berryman's *Homage to Mistress Bradstreet* (1956).

SOR JUANA INÉS DE LA CRUZ (1648/51–1695)   Juana de Asbaje y Ramírez was born in San Miguel de Nepantla, where she learned to speak Nahua (Nahuatl), the Aztec language of the village, as well as Spanish. She was the daughter of a Spaniard and a Mexican woman. She was to become the first and the most important literary figure in the Spanish-speaking New World. As a young girl she was precocious in reading, writing, and literary composition. At the viceroy's court in Mexico City she astonished the scholars with her knowledge of philosophy, science, mathematics, literature, theology, and music. Being a "daughter of the church," a euphemism for illegitimate, limited her career at the court and her marriage possibilities. She joined the order of Saint Jerome. As a nun Sor Juana found the time to study and write. With the help of the wife of the viceroy, her works were published in Mexico and Spain. However, her love poems brought a reprimand from the bishop of Puebla, who ordered her to follow Paul's dictum and to be silent. She responded with a letter, which is the world's first *A Room of One's Own*, in which she strongly defends women's right in all personal and social areas. The letter is also an autobiography. After the incident, she sold her library of some four thousand volumes and went to work for the poor in the provinces and died attending her sick sisters in the convent during an epidemic. Sor Juana used all the devices of metaphysical baroque poetry in her *First Dream,* which is the most sustained long philosophical poem in the Spanish language.

PHILLIS WHEATLEY (1753–1784)   Wheatley was the first black American woman to publish a book in English in North America. She was brought to America at the age of eight from West Africa on the slave ship *Phillis.* Through the effort of her master's daughter, Mary Wheatley, she obtained a full education in the classics and began to write poetry when she was twelve. Her master's son took her to London in 1773, where her book *Poems on Various Subjects, Religious and Moral* was published. She became well known in the revolutionary period, and as a result of her poetry she was invited to a personal visit in 1775 with George Washington at his headquarters in Cambridge. Eventually freed, she married a freeman, had three children, and died at age thirty-one; her third child was buried with her. Wheatley wrote largely in the neoclassical heroic couplet of Pope, Dryden, and Swift. In an era when early deaths from natural or violent causes were common, her poems are often elegiac, speaking of mortality and how to survive the loss of one's loved ones.

ANNETTE VON DROSTE-HÜLSHOFF (1797–1848)   From a family of Westphalian nobility, Droste-Hülshoff wrote poems often of a pessimistic nature, centering on the passage of time. Literary scholars have suggested that her poor eyesight gave her a very special vision of nature.

WU ZAO (Wu Tsao) (19th century)   The daughter of a merchant with whom she had little in common, Wu Zao wrote love poems to women lovers and to courtesans. Some of her poems reflect philosophically on the past, on China's great poets, and on the misty temporality of memory.

ELIZABETH BARRETT BROWNING (1806–1861)   At the age of twelve Elizabeth Barrett wrote an epic in four parts, *The Battle of Marathon,* which her father had published. A semi-invalid, she eloped with Robert Browning. Unforgiven by her father, the Brownings went to Italy, where, writing and entertaining literary friends, including Nathaniel Hawthorne and Julia Ward Howe, she enjoyed great success with *Sonnets from the Portuguese* (1850). She had a keen social conscience and was a champion of the Italian struggle for independence from Austria, and for women's rights, child labor laws, and the abolition of slavery.

BIBI HAYATI (d. 1853)   Born in the early part of the nineteenth century into a family devoted to Sufism, in Kerman, a province of Persia, Hayati was raised by her brother, who guided her to the contemplative life. As a young person she was initiated into the rites of Sufism and thereafter, as a rhapsodist, followed the Sufi path (*tariqat*), which included a knowledge of the thirteenth-century Sufi philosophers Ibn al-Farid and Ibn al-Arabi and the mystical poet Jalaludin Rumi. She married Nur 'Ali Shah, a Sufi master, who asked her to compose a *divan* (or collection) of poems.

CHARLOTTE BRONTË (1816–1855)   Charlotte Brontë was born in Yorkshire, England, and was the daughter of an Irish clergyman. She grew up on the moors, which color her poems. In 1854 she married and the next year died of illness following childbirth. Her novel *Jane Eyre*, published under the name of Currer Bell, made her famous. Her atmospheric poetry strongly influenced Emily Dickinson.

EMILY DICKINSON (1830–1886)   Dickinson was born and died in Amherst, Massachusetts. Her grandfather founded evangelical Amherst College in reaction to liberal Harvard. Her father was a member of the U.S. House of Representatives and brought the railroad to Amherst. Emily Dickinson attended Mount Holyoke Female Seminary, then also an evangelical institution. After a year she withdrew, unwilling to "convert" through a profession of faith. Dickinson read widely and was influenced by the Bible, Shakespeare, the prosody of Protestant hymns, Keats, and Robert and Elizabeth Barrett Browning. In the late 1860s she began to withdraw from society. Her withdrawal was not complete, however, since she carried on an extensive correspondence with her family and friends, in which she often included poems, her private publications. She turned for advice to her friend Thomas Wentworth Higginson, editor of the *Atlantic Monthly*, who failed to recognize her genius. After her death he and Mabel Loomis Todd transcribed her poems, "correcting" her innovative slant rhymes and doctoring her metaphors, producing a bowdlerized version, which was standard until 1955 when Thomas H. Johnson largely restored the original texts. Dickinson spent most of her life at home in Amherst, but her circumference expands into the vastness of the universe. Her poems deal with questions of faith posed by her nineteenth-century milieu and transcend place and era. She is one of the greatest spiritual and visionary poets of the world. Modern poetry begins with Emily Dickinson and Walt Whitman, who between them gave us the means and spirit of our contemporary poetic world.

ROSALÍA DE CASTRO (1837–1885)   Rosalía de Castro came from Santiago de Compostela in Galicia, Spain. An illegitimate child, she grew up learning Spanish and Galician, a dialect of Portuguese, and wrote most of her poems in Galician. After she separated from her husband, a historian with whom she had five children, her life was harsh and isolated. Her poems are pessimistic, sonorous, and given to dark dream.

ELSE LASKER-SCHÜLER (1869–1945)   Born in Elberfeld, Germany, Lasker-Schüler was an early German expressionist poet, and her circle included George Trakl and the painter Franz Marc. When her work was banned by the Nazis, she fled to Switzerland and later to Jerusalem, where she died. Among her finest poems are those with biblical themes.

YOSANO AKIKO (1878–1942)   A Japanese feminist who spoke out against Japanese expansionism, Yosano Akido was a prolific writer of poetry, essays, and novels. Her first book was *Tangled Hair*, a collection of tanka. She was both a traditional poet of the tanka and a modern poet.

H.D. (1886–1961)   H.D. was born in Bethlehem, Pennsylvania, was raised Moravian and Quaker, attended Bryn Mawr College, and was a classicist all her life. In 1911 she went to England and thereafter remained in Europe. With Ezra Pound she was an early imagist, but she soon developed a deep knowledge of Greek, Christian, and Near Eastern religions, which affected her poems. She wrote abundantly—poetry, fiction, essays, a play—and translated Greek drama. She also had a brief career as a European film actress. Essential to her development was her relationship with Freud. She recorded her months of psychoanalysis in *Tribute to Freud* (1956). She wrote *Trilogy* in London during World War II. The three long visionary poems that *Trilogy* comprises—*The Walls Do Not Fall* (1944), *Tribute to the Angels* (1945), and *The Flowering of the Rod* (1946)—synthesize H.D.'s vast knowledge of esoteric spiritual practices, the Egyptian and Greek pagan religions, and the Judeo-Christian traditions, especially the Bible, which was one of her main sources. She received a copy of her last masterpiece, *Helen in Egypt,* the day before her death.

MARIANNE MOORE (1887–1972)   Born in St. Louis, Missouri (a year before T. S. Eliot was born in the same city), Moore went to Bryn Mawr

College. She had various jobs teaching stenography, typing, and commercial law at Carlisle Indian School and worked at the New York Public Library. For years she was editor of *The Dial*. In 1951 her *Collected Poems* appeared, with an introduction by Eliot. Her *Complete Poems* came out in 1966. She also translated *The Fables of La Fontaine* (1954). Often taking found passages from newspapers, in poems of strict syllabic meter, she presented an acute vision of the ordinary, which, as in "The Steeple-Jack," she made into spiritual parable. Of her borrowings from contemporary life, which she creatively made her own, she wrote in her notebook: "A good stealer is *ipso facto* a good inventor."

ANNA AKHMATOVA (1889–1966)   Born in Odessa, Akhmatova lived at the imperial summer residence at Tsarskoye Selo near St. Petersburg until she was sixteen. She went to law school and in 1910 married the poet and critic Nikolai Gumilev. The next year she spent in Paris, where the then unknown painter Modigliani did sixteen portrait drawings of her. Her second book of poems, *Chyotki (Rosary)* (1914), brought her fame. With the poet Osip Mandelstam she was associated with Acmeism, a movement to clarify the vagueness of symbolism. She divorced in 1918, and three years later Gumilev was executed. In 1922 she published *Anno Domini MCMXXI*, her last book before the Soviets silenced her. She earned her living, poorly, through translation. With World War II she was evacuated from Leningrad to Tashkent, but she was permitted to publish again. In 1946 she was again attacked by the Writers Union, and her son was arrested. After Stalin's death she was rehabilitated and her son released from prison. In 1965 she was given an honorary degree by Oxford University. By the time of her death she had a new circle of protégés, including Joseph Brodsky, and was recognized as the Soviet Union's foremost poet.

NELLY SACHS (1891–1970)   Born in Berlin, Nelly Sachs hid from the Nazis during the Third Reich. With other Jews she escaped to Stockholm, where she spent the rest of her life. She published many books of poems, wrote a verse play and a ballad book. Her works have been widely translated. She was awarded the Nobel Prize for literature in 1966.

ALFONSINA STORNI (1892–1938)   Born in Capriasca, Switzerland, Storni lived in Argentina from the age of four. After her father's death she worked as an actress to help support her family. In 1910 she published her first book of poems and moved to Buenos Aires, where she worked as a journalist and teacher in state schools. In 1923 she was named professor of literature at the Normal School of Modern Languages. In 1938 breast cancer recurred and she drowned herself in the ocean at Mar del Plata. Storni developed into a poet of surprise, ironic strength, and grim vision. Her works include *La Inquietud del Vosal* (*The Disquiet of the Rosebush*) (1916), *Selected Poems* (1940), and *Poetry* (1948).

EDITH SÖDERGRAN (1892–1923)   Södergran was born in St. Petersburg but used Swedish at home, since her family came from the Swedish-speaking region of Finland. Educated at a German school, her first poems were in German. At the age of sixteen she contracted tuberculosis, a disease that had taken her father two years earlier. Her family returned to Raivola in Finland, and during World War I, when civil war resulted after Finland declared its independence from Russia, she experienced hunger. Her first books of poems were greeted with scorn, since she wrote in free verse at a time when only formal verse was recognized as poetry in conservative Swedish circles. When invited to Helsinki by Ola Hansson, a critic who wrote a good review of her work, she was pleased but had to decline: "Sleeplessness, tuberculosis, no money. We live by selling furniture and household goods." She died on Midsummer's Day, 1923.

MARINA TSVETAYEVA (1892–1941)   Born in Moscow, the daughter of a musician mother and a father who was a professor of art history at Moscow University and founder of the Pushkin Museum, Tsvetayeva was educated in boarding schools in Switzerland and Germany. She married Sergei Efron. With the revolution she sided with the White Army and emigrated to Prague and then to Paris. In Paris she was ostracized by *émigrés* for supporting the poetry of Vladimir Mayakovsky. Persuaded by Boris Pasternak to return to the Soviet Union, she went back in 1939. Her husband was arrested and executed, her son killed in the war. The Soviet authorities exiled her to Elabuga, where, friendless and unable to find work, she hanged herself. Her poems are usually short-lined stanzas in sequences reaching an amazing crescendo of candor and defiance. She is one of the decisive voices of Europe whose poems mirror the century. A passionately intelligent and original poet, her voice has been translated into the world's languages.

ANONYMOUS HAWAIIAN   Armand Schwerner's reexpressions of Hawaiian poetry are based on the transcriptions of anthropologists.

ANONYMOUS INNUIT   This women's lament song ends in a blank vision of whiteness in which the inland of the mind and the earth are the same.

LORINE NIEDECKER (1903–1970)   Born in Fort Atkinson, Wisconsin, Niedecker was educated at Beloit College, then did freelance writing and editing. Disenchanted with the city, she lived for the next twenty years on Black Hawk Island on Lake Koshkonong, earning her living by cleaning the kitchen and scrubbing floors in a local hospital. She married a housepainter in 1951 and for the next eighteen years lived in the poorest section of Milwaukee. She returned to Black Hawk Island the last year of her life. In the objectivist tradition, Cid Corman, her literary executor, calls Niedecker's poetry "quiet music." In the tradition of Pound and Williams, Niedecker was a master of the condensed poem, of the image that illumines and quietly explodes with sound and meaning. *From this Condensery: The Complete Writing of Lorine Niedecker* came out in 1985.

BETTI ALVER (b. 1906)   Alver was the leading woman poet in Estonia. Her tragicomic treatment of spiritual life often takes on a science fiction imagination when heavenly beings invade the earth. Her books include *Dust and Fire* (1936) and *Starry Hour* (1936).

THÉRÈSE PLANTIER (b. 1911)   Born in Nîmes, France, Thérèse Plantier began her career in Paris, associated with postwar surrealists. Later she returned to the southern France of her youth. A prolific poet, she has translated contemporary British poets into French.

MURIEL RUKEYSER (1913–1980)   From New York City, Rukeyser was educated at Vassar College and Columbia University. She was in Spain as a journalist when the civil war began in 1936. Later she was on the faculty of Sarah Lawrence College. Her first book, *Theory of Flight*, received the Yale Younger Poets Award. She wrote prose and children's books and translated the poems of Octavio Paz, *Sun Stone* (1962). Her *Collected Poems* appeared in 1978 and *A Muriel Rukeyser Reader* in 1994.

JULIA DE BURGOS (1914–1953)   Born in 1914 in Carolina, Puerto Rico, and eldest of thirteen children, Julia de Burgos went to the University of Puerto Rico and taught school in Naranjito. After her first book came out in 1938, *Poem in Twenty Furrows*, she taught at the University of Havana. In 1940 she moved to New York. Her short and productive life was also tormented and chaotic, fraught with poverty and alcoholism. Her *Collected Works* appeared in 1961.

RUTH STONE (b. 1915)   Born in Roanoke, Virginia, Stone was a journalist for the *Indianapolis Star* and editor at Wesleyan University Press, and has been a visiting professor at many universities, including Virginia, Brandeis, Wisconsin, and Radcliffe. She holds a distinguished chair in poetry at SUNY Binghamton. Ruth Stone has been widely honored, including winning the Shelley Award from the Poetry Society of America and being twice the recipient of a Guggenheim Fellowship. She is the author of ten books of poetry, her most recent volume being *Ordinary Words: Selected Poems* (1999).

ANNE HÉBERT (b. 1916)   Hébert was born and raised in Sainte Catherine, a village twenty miles from Quebec City. Her reputation was established with the publication of *Le tombeau des rois* (The Tomb of the Kings) in 1953. Her novel *Kamouraska* was made into a film. She has written for film, television, and the theater. Her common subject is repressed and demoralized women in a surreal domestic setting. A leading poet in the French language, Anne Hébert lives in Paris.

GWENDOLYN BROOKS (b. 1917)   A prolific poet, novelist, memoirist, and anthologist, Brooks is a lifelong Chicagoan. Her more than twenty books of poetry include *Children Coming Home* (1991), *Blacks* (1987), *The Near-Johannesburg Boy and Other Poems* (1986), *To Disembark* (1981), *The Bean Eaters* (1960), and *A Street in Bronzeville* (1945). In 1949 her book of poems *Annie Allen* made her the first African American to win the Pulitzer Prize. Among her many honors and awards are her tenures as Poet Laureate of Illinois (succeeding Carl Sandburg) and Consultant in Poetry to the Library of Congress, as well as the establishment of the Gwendolyn Brooks Center for Black Literature and Creative Writing at Chicago State University.

GLORIA FUERTES (b. 1918)   From Madrid, Fuertes has worked as a teacher, librarian, and editor. She spent three years in the United States, where she taught Spanish literature. Her first book, published in 1954, was *Anthology of Poetics and Poems of the Slums*. Her poems are concerned with daily life, lesbian love, and human rights in a society that until 1975 was highly repressive. One of Spain's best-known poets after the civil war, she has been translated into English by Philip Levine. Her work frequently appears in *American Poetry Review* and other distinguished periodicals.

MARY ELLEN SOLT (b. 1920) Solt was born in Gilmore City, Iowa. She is a pioneer theorist and anthologist and the premier poet of the international concrete poetry movement. As a critic she has written extensively about her friend William Carlos Williams. She was the editor of *Concrete Poetry: A World View* (1968), the most comprehensive anthology of concrete poetry and theory, and her own poems reveal far-reaching interests, from moon rocketry to semiotics. Her poems have been published widely and exhibited in most countries in Europe, in Tokyo, and at the Museum of Modern Art in New York. Some of her books are *Flowers in Concrete* (1966), *A Trilogy of Rain* (1970), *Words and Spaces* (1957–1977). Her nonconcrete poetry (what she calls her linear poetry), a national secret, places her among the outstanding poets of her generation.

DENISE LEVERTOV (1923–1998) Born in Ilford, Essex, England, Denise Levertov served as a nurse during World War II. In 1947 she came to the United States. Originally part of the Black Mountain group, she was a professor at Tufts College, a scholar at the Radcliffe Institute, and visiting professor at leading universities. She was a prolific poet, a translator of contemporary French and East Indian poetry, and the poetry editor of the *Nation*.

WISLAWA SZYMBORSKA (b. 1923) Szymborska lives in Kraków, Poland. Early in her career she was condemned for not following Stalinist critics, who opposed her aesthetic tendencies. Winner of the Nobel Prize for literature in 1996, her *Poems New and Collected 1957–1997* were published in 1998 in English, containing work from seven books. In her Nobel acceptance address, Wislawa Szymborska states that she dreams of chatting with the great poet Ecclesiastes and asking him what thing under the sun he is planning to work on. She tells him, as she tells us, that everything has not been said, that every day the poet says the unknown anew.

INGEBORG BACHMANN (1926–1973) Born in Kalgenfurt, Austria, Bachmann spent her childhood under the Nazis, and recalled Hitler's troops arriving in her hometown: "It was so horrifying that my memory begins with this day . . . the origin of my first fear of death." She studied at the universities of Innsbruck and Graz and in 1950 at the University of Vienna, where she wrote a dissertation on Martin Heidegger. She moved to Italy but worked as a journalist internationally, living at times in Paris, Munich, London, and New York. She won Germany's highest award for literature, the Buchner Prize, after which she wrote only fiction. In her apartment in Rome, she fell asleep in bed with a burning cigarette, the mattress caught fire, and she died three weeks later from burns.

ANNE SEXTON (1928–1974) Born in Newton, Massachusetts, Sexton grew up in Wellesley and was educated at Garland Junior College and studied with Robert Lowell at Boston University. She was a scholar at the Radcliffe Institute and won the Pulitzer Prize for her volume *Live or Die* in 1967. Among her many honors were the Robert Frost Fellowship at the Vermont Bread Loaf Writers' Conference and three honorary Doctor of Arts and Letters degrees. Her life was plagued by mental illness, and she began writing poetry as therapy. Like Emily Dickinson's, her poems are often a conflicted dialogue with God. In her late work Sexton's poems center on "the awful rowing toward god," the title of a book published in the last year of her life. In 1974 she committed suicide. Her books include *To Bedlam and Part Way Back* (1960), which first brought her fame, *Love Poems* (1969), *The Book of Folly* (1972), *The Death Notebooks* (1974), *45 Mercy Street* (1976), and *The Complete Poems* (1981).

SYLVIA PLATH (1932–1963) Born in Boston, Plath went to Smith College. While in Cambridge she and her friend Anne Sexton studied with Robert Lowell, who wrote a foreword to her posthumous collection *Ariel*. As a Fulbright Scholar in Cambridge, she met the English poet Ted Hughes, whom she married. They returned to America where Plath taught at Smith for a year. They returned to England where her two children were born. Her first book of poems, *The Colossus*, was published in England in 1960. In 1962 she separated from Hughes, moving from Devon to London. She committed suicide on February 11, 1963. Her posthumous *Collected Poems* was awarded the Pulitzer Prize in 1982. From the beginning her poems show a classical and desperate clarity; the startling and brutal images crowd elliptically in both her closed and open forms. In the last months of her life she wrote searing poems with what Hughes called her "crackling verbal energy." Among her other publications are her novel, *The Bell Jar* (1963), and her journals and short stories.

INGRID JONKER (1933–1965) Born in South Africa, Jonker traveled extensively in Europe. She was an early strong opponent of apartheid, which led to many personal difficulties with government authorities and with her father. She committed suicide in her thirty-first year. Ingrid Jonker wrote in Afrikaans.

LUCILLE CLIFTON (b. 1936) Clifton, a poet, children's book writer, and memoirist, is Distinguished Professor of Humanities at St. Mary's College of Maryland, and her books include *The Terrible Stories* (1996), *The Book of Light* (1993), *Quilting: Poems 1987–1990* (1991), *Next: New Poems* (1989), *Good Woman: Poems and a Memoir 1969–1980* (1989), *Good Times* (1969), and *Generations: A Memoir* (1976). She has received many awards, including the Juniper Prize for poetry, two creative writing fellowships from the National Endowment for the Arts, and an Emmy Award from the American Academy of Television Arts and Sciences.

BELLA AKHMADULINA (b. 1937) A Moscovite of Tartar and Italian descent, Akhmadulina attended the Gorky Institute of Literature, from which she was expelled. Her first volume of poems, *String* (1962), was strongly influenced by Akhmatova and was criticized by the government as "superfluous and too intimate." Although she was allowed to publish in magazines, she could not join the Writer's Union as a poet but was finally permitted to do translations and earn her living. A formal poet, she has the freshness of daring free verse. In recent years she has moved closer to Marina Tsvetayeva's clipped, passionate verse. She is widely translated into many languages.

LINDA GREGG (b. 1942) Born in Suffern, New York, Gregg grew up in northern California and was educated at San Francisco State University. Her poems have been influenced by Chinese and Greek poetry, and especially by her extended residences in Greece. Among her books are *Too Bright to See* (1981), *Alma* (1985), *The Sacraments of Desire* (1991), and *Chosen by the Lion* (1994). The landscapes and presences in her Greek poems guide us over the border into the ineffable.

JENI COUSZYN (b. 1942) Born and educated in South Africa, Couszyn moved first to England, then to Victoria, British Columbia, Toronto, and back to London. Her many books include *Christmas in Africa* (1975), *The Happiness Bird* (1978), and *Life by Drowning I* (1983). She is the editor of *The Bloodaxe Book of Contemporary Women Poets* (1985). Accomplished and wildly imaginative in her imagery and flow, Couszyn is one of the brightest voices from contemporary Africa.

TESS GALLAGHER (b. 1943) Gallagher, a poet, essayist, novelist, and playwright, was born in Port Angeles, Washington. She was educated at the University of Washington (where she studied creative writing with Theodore Roethke) and at the University of Iowa. Her honors include a fellowship from the Guggenheim Foundation, two National Endowment of the Arts Awards, the Maxine Cushing Gray Foundation Award, and the Elliston Award for "Best Book of Poetry Published by a Small Press" for the collection *Instructions to the Double* (1976). In 1984, she published the collection *Willingly*, which consists of poems written to and about her third husband, author Raymond Carver. She has also written two books of fiction, *The Lover of Horses and Other Stories* and *At the Owl-Woman Saloon*. Gallagher's other books of poetry include *Amplitude: New and Selected Poems* (1987), the elegiac *Moon Crossing Bridge* (1992), from which "Wake" is taken, published after Carver's death, and *My Black Horse: New and Selected Poems* (1995). Gallagher has taught at many universities and lives in Port Angeles, Washington.

LOUISE GLÜCK (b. 1943)   Born in New York City, Glück's volumes of poetry include *The House on Marshland* (1975); *The Triumph of Achilles* (1985); *Wild Iris* (1992), for which she received the Pulitzer Prize; and *Meadowlands* (1996). Her book *Proofs and Theories: Essays on Poetry* appeared in 1993. She teaches at Williams College.

YONA WALLACH (1944–1985)   A native of Israel, Wallach used the Hebrew language as no one had before. Her translator, Linda Zisquit, notes that she exhibits an exhilaration and garrulousness in her poetry, an unleashing of energy and excitement in the free use of what had in the past been restricted. She was blatantly sexual, filled with "a wild light" in keeping with her book's title. She was deeply religious, with an outrageous personal mysticism. She died of breast cancer at age forty-one.

LINDA HOGAN (b. 1947)   Hogan, of the Chickasaw Tribe, has played a prominent role in the development of contemporary Native American poetry, particularly in its relationship to environmental and antinuclear issues. She is the author of the poetry books *The Book of Medicines* (1993) and the award-winning *Seeing Through the Sun* (1985); a play entitled *A Piece of Moon*, which garnered the Five Civilized Tribes Museum Award for drama; and the novels *Mean Spirit* (1992), which portrays the illegal reclamation of oil-rich Osage reservation land by the U.S. government during the 1920s, and *Solar Storms* (1993).

OLGA BROUMAS (b. 1949)   Broumas, born in Syros, Greece, won the Yale Younger Poets Award from Yale University Press for *Beginning with O* (1977). She is the author of *Soie Sauvage* (1980), *Perpetua* (1989), and, with T Begley, *Sappho's Gymnasium* (1994), a Sapphic sequence of some one hundred eighty poems in the oral ecstatic tradition, which returns to the traditions of Sappho and Odysseus Elytis, the Nobel-prize-winning Greek poet whom Broumas has translated extensively. Her other honors include fellowships from the National Endowment for the Arts and the Guggenheim Foundation. She is Fannie Hurst Professor at Brandeis University.

LILIANA URSU (b. 1949)   Liliana Ursu was born in Romania, and her poems have been published in *The Sky Behind the Forest: Selected Poems* (1997).

ANNE CARSON (b. 1950)   Carson is the author of a philosophical medi-tation on love and longing, *Eros the Bittersweet* (1986), whose title, de-rived from a Sappho fragment, points to her classicist background. A professor of classics at McGill University, Anne Carson has emerged as a fresh, ingenious, outstanding voice among contemporary poets who takes her knowledge into a debate with God. Her books of poetry, *Glass, Irony, and God* and *Plainwater,* appeared in 1995.

DEBORAH DIGGES (b. 1950)   Deborah Digges's books of poems include *Vesper Sparrows* and *Late in the Millennium* (1989). She has also pub-lished a memoir, *Fugitive Spring* (1992). She has received fellowships from the Ingram Merrill Foundation, the National Endowment for the Arts, and the Guggenheim Foundation. She currently lives in Massa-chusetts and is Associate Professor of English at Tufts University.

CAROLYN FORCHÉ (b. 1950)   Forché's first poetry collection, *Gathering the Tribes* (1976), won the Yale Younger Poets Award from Yale Univer-sity Press. She received a Guggenheim Foundation Fellowship, which enabled her to live in El Salvador for two years, where she worked as a human rights activist. Her experiences there informed her second book, *The Country Between Us* (1982), which received the Poetry Society of America's Alice Fay di Castagnola Award and was chosen as the Lamont Selection of the Academy of American Poets. Her translations of the work of Salvadoran, exiled poet Claribel Alegria are collected in *Flowers From the Volcano* (1983). Her anthology, *Against Forgetting: Twentieth Century Poetry of Witness* (1993) is a collection of poetry in English and in translation by poets who endured conditions of social, historical, and political extremity during the twentieth century. Her third book of poetry, *The Angel of History* (1994), received the Los Angeles Times

Book Award. Forché has held three fellowships from The National Endowment for the Arts, and she received a Lannan Foundation Literary Award. She teaches in the Master of Fine Arts Program in Poetry at George Mason University in Virginia.

JORIE GRAHAM (b. 1951)   Jorie Graham was born in New York City. She is the author of seven collections of poetry, including *The Errancy* (1997); *The Dream of the Unified Field: Selected Poems 1974–1994*, which won the 1996 Pulitzer Prize for poetry; *Materialism* (1993); *Region of Unlikeness* (1991); *The End of Beauty* (1987); *Erosion* (1983); and *Hybrids of Plants and Ghosts* (1980). She has also edited two anthologies, *Earth Took of Earth: 100 Great Poems of the English Language* (1996) and *The Best American Poetry 1990*. Her honors include a John D. and Catherine T. MacArthur Fellowship and the Morton Dauwen Zabel Award from the American Academy and Institute of Arts and Letters. A member of the permanent faculty of the University of Iowa Writers' Workshop, she lives in Iowa City with her husband and daughter.

JOY HARJO (b. 1951)   Born in Oklahoma, of the Creek Tribe, Joy Harjo has published *She Had Some Horses* (1983), *Secrets from the Center of the World* (1989), *In Mad Love and War* (1990), and *The Woman Who Fell from the Sky* (1994). She also plays the saxophone. Her band, Poetic Justice, combines elements of poetry, tribal music, jazz, reggae, and rock. She teaches creative writing and Native American Literature at the University of Arizona.

BRENDA HILLMAN (b. 1951)   Hillman's sources are as diverse as her childhood in Brazil and her immersion in Gnosticism. She has published five books: *White Dress* (1985), *Fortress* (1989), *Death Tractates* (1992), *Bright Existence* (1993), and *Loose Sugar* (1997). She has received two Pushcart Prizes, a Guggenheim Foundation Fellowship, and the Delmore Schwartz Memorial Award for Poetry. She teaches poetry writing at St. Mary's College in California and lives in Kensington, California with her husband, poet Robert Hass.

SHU DING (Shu Ting) (b. 1952)   Born in Shanghai, Shu Ding has been published widely in English and other languages, including in *Out of the Howling Storm: Contemporary Chinese Poetry*, edited by Tony Barnstone. She was one of the leaders of the "Misty School," which represented a singular attempt to move Chinese verse from socialist realism propaganda in poetry. She is one of China's leading poets.

ANITA ENDREZZE (b. 1952)   Born in California, of Yaqui and European ancestry, Endrezze is a poet, short story writer, and painter. Her books include *at the helm of twilight* (poems), *The Humming of Stars and Bees and Waves* (poems and stories), and *Throwing Fire at the Sun, Water at the Moon*, a look at family and tribal history.

AMINA SAÏD (b. 1953)   Born in Tunis, Amina Saïd has published several books of poetry, including *Paysage, nuit friable* (1980) and *Métamorphose et la vague* (1985).

RACHIDA MADANI (b. 1953)   Madani was born in Tangier. The author of several books of poetry, she published *Femme je suis* in 1981.

ROSANNA WARREN (b. 1954)   Warren studied painting before she began her studies in literature. Now a professor in the University Professors Program and the Department of English at Boston University, she is a poet, fiction writer, translator, editor, and scholar. Her many honors include a Lila Wallace Readers' Digest Award, a Lamont Poetry Prize, Ingram Merrill Grants, a Guggenheim Fellowship, and a Yaddo Fellowship. Her books include *The Joey Story* (1963) (a work of fiction) and three volumes of poetry: *Snow Day* (1981), *Each Leaf Shines Separate* (1984), and *Stained Glass* (1993).

LOUISE ERDRICH (b. 1955)   Erdrich, a poet, memoirist, children's book writer, and best-selling novelist, was raised in North Dakota and is of German and Ojibwa descent. Her grandfather was tribal chair of the Turtle Mountain Band of Ojibwa. Her books include the poetry books *Jacklight* (1984) and *Baptism of Desire* (1989); the novels *Love Medicine* (1984), *The Beet Queen* (1986); *Tracks* (1989), *The Bingo Palace* (1995), *Tales of Burning Love* (1996), and *The Antelope Wife and Other Short Stories* (1998); a memoir of motherhood, *The Blue Jay's Dance: A Birth Year* (1996); and a children's book, *Grandmother's Pigeon* (1996).

ALIKI BARNSTONE (b. 1956)   Barnstone teaches at the University of Nevada, Las Vegas. Her most recent book of poems, *Madly in Love* (1997), was nominated for the Pulitzer Prize.

T BEGLEY (b. 1956)   A poet and teacher, T Begley lives and writes in Cape Cod, Massachusetts. Her work has appeared in journals and her collaborations with Olga Broumas include *Sappho's Gymnasium and Open Papers: Selected Essays of Odysseas Elytis*, and *Ithaca-Little Summer in Winter*. In addition to writing poetry, Begley has presented installation and performance pieces.

Lucie Brock-Broido (b. 1956)   Brock-Broido's highly praised books of poems are *A Hunger* (1988) and *The Master Letters* (1995). She is director of poetry in the MFA program of the School of the Arts at Columbia University and lives in New York City and Cambridge, Massachusetts.

CREDITS

Every effort has been made to trace the copyright holders of material in this book. The editor apologizes if any work has been used without permission and would be glad to be told of anyone who has not been consulted.

The editor wishes to thank Chou Ping, Elene Kolb, Usha Nilsson, and Sun Chu-chin for their assistance with translations by Aliki Barnstone, Willis Barnstone, and Tony Barnstone.

Anonymous Egyptian. "I find my love fishing" translated by Noel Stock and Ezra Pound from *Love Poems of Ancient Egypt*. Copyright © 1962 by Noel Stock and Ezra Pound. Reprinted by permission of New Directions Publishing Corp.

Patacara. "Patacara Speaks" from *The Songs of the Sons and Daughters of Buddha* translated by Andrew Schelling & Anne Waldman, © 1996. Reprinted by arrangement with Shambhala Publications, Inc., Boston.

Sangha. Reprinted from *The First Buddhist Women: Translations and Commentary on the Therigatha* (1991) by Susan Murcott with permission of Parallax Press, Berkeley, California.

Sakula. Reprinted from *The First Buddhist Women: Translations and Commentary on the Therigatha* (1991) by Susan Murcott with permission of Parallax Press, Berkeley, California.

Dantika. "As I left my daytime resting place" reprinted from *The First Buddhist Women: Translations and Commentary on the Therigatha* (1991) by Susan Murcott with permission of Parallax Press, Berkeley, California.

Nandutta. "Nanduttara" from *The Songs of the Sons and Daughters of Buddha* translated by Andrew Schelling & Anne Waldman, © 1996. Reprinted by arrangement with Shambhala Publications, Inc., Boston.

Anonymous Buddhist Sister. "An Anonymous Sister Speaks" from *The Songs of the Sons and Daughters of Buddha* translated by Andrew Schelling & Anne Waldman, © 1996. Reprinted by arrangement with Shambhala Publications, Inc., Boston.

Sisupacala. "Sisupacala Speaks with Mara" from *The Songs of the Sons and Daughters of Buddha* translated by Andrew Schelling & Anne Waldman, © 1996. Reprinted by arrangement with Shambhala Publications, Inc., Boston.

Govindasvamin. "Holy sixth day" appeared in *The Peacock's Egg: Love Poems from Ancient India*, translated by W. S. Merwin and J. Moussaif Masson (New York: North Point Press, 1981). Translation copyright © 1981 by W. S. Merwin and J. Moussaif Masson. Reprinted by permission of Georges Borchardt, Inc.

Anonymous Sanskrit Songs. "When he comes back," "My husband," and "He who stole my virginity" appeared in *The Peacock's Egg: Love Poems from Ancient India*, translated by W. S. Merwin and J. Moussaif Masson (New York: North Point Press, 1981). Translation copyright © 1981 by W. S. Merwin and J. Moussaif Masson. Reprinted by permission of Georges Borchardt, Inc.

Anonymous Indian. Excerpts from *Not Far from the River: Poems from the Gatha Saptasati* © 1983 and 1990 by David Ray. Reprinted by permission of Copper Canyon Press, Post Office Box 271, Port Townsend, WA 98368.

Yeshe Tsogyel. Excerpt from *Sky Dancer: The Secret Life and Songs of Lady Yeshe Tsogyel* by Keith Dowman. By permission of Snow Lion Publications.

Wu Cailuan. All poems from *Immortal Sisters: Secret Teachings of Taoist Women*, translated and edited by Thomas Cleary, copyright © 1989, 1996. Reprinted with permission of North Atlantic Books, Berkeley, California, USA.

Yu Xuanji. "At the End of Spring," "Regretful Thoughts," "For Hidden Mist Pavillion," and "Answering Li Ying Who Showed Me His Poems about Summer Fishing," translated by Geoffrey Waters, appeared in *A*

Anna Akhmatova. "How Can You Look at the Neva" from *Poems of Akhmatova*, translated by Stanley Kunitz & Max Hayward, Houghton Mifflin Co. Copyright © 1997 by Stanley Kunitz. Reprinted by permission of Darhansoff and Verrill Literary Agents. "Until I Collapse" and "The Summer Garden," from *The Complete Poems of Anna Akhmatova*, translated by Judith Hemschemeyer, edited by Roberta Reeder. Copyright © 1990, 1992, 1997 by Judith Hemschemeyer. Reprinted by permission of Zephyr Press. "Lot's Wife," translated by Richard Wilbur, from *Walking to Sleep: New Poems and Translations*, copyright © 1969 and renewed 1997 by Richard Wilbur, reprinted by permission of Harcourt Inc.

Marina Tsvetayeva. "Bent with worry," "Poems for Blok," "We shall not escape Hell," "Where you are I can reach you," "Verses about Moscow," from *The Selected Poems of Marina Tsvetaeva* by Marina Tsvetaeva, translated by Elaine Feinstein, copyright © 1971, 1981 by Elaine Feinstein. Used by permission of Dutton, a division of Penguin Putnam Inc., and Sheil-Land Associates, Inc.

Anonymous Hawaiian. "Dirge" translated by Armand Schwerner appeared in *A Book of Women Poets from Antiquity to Now*, edited by Aliki Barnstone and Willis Barnstone (Schocken Books, 1980).

Lorine Niedecker. All poems copyright © 1999 Cid Corman, literary executor of the Lorine Niedecker Estate. By permission of Cid Corman.

Thérèse Plantier. "Overdue Balance Sheet," translated by Maxine Kumin and Judith Kumin. Copyright © Maxine Kumin and Judith Kumin. By permission of the translators.

Muriel Rukeyser. "Waiting for Icarus" from *A Muriel Rukeyser Reader*, edited by Jan Heller Levi, W. W. Norton & Co. Copyright © 1994 by Jan Heller Levi. Copyright © 1935, 1938, 1939, 1942, 1944, 1948, 1951, 1958, 1962, 1968, 1973, 1976 by Muriel Rukeyser. By permission of International Creative Management, Inc.

Ruth Stone. All poems by permission of the author.

Anne Hébert. "Bread is Born," translated by Maxine Kumin. © Maxine Kumin. Reprinted by permission of the translator.

Gwendolyn Brooks. All poems from Blacks by Gwendolyn Brooks, copyright © 1987 by Gwendolyn Brooks. Reprinted by permission of Third World Press Inc., Chicago, Ill.

Mary Ellen Solt. "Forsythia" from *Flowers in Concrete*, 1966. By permission of the author.

Denise Levertov. "The Life of Others" by Denise Levertov, from *Candles in Babylon*. Copyright © 1982 by Denise Levertov. Reprinted by permission of New Directions Publishing Corp. Originally published in *The Freeing of the Dust*, Bloodaxe Books, and is reprinted here by permission of Laurence Pollinger Limited.

Wislawa Szymborska. "I Am Too Near" by Wislawa Szymborska, from *Postwar Polish Poetry* by Czeslaw Milosz. Translation copyright 1965 by Czeslaw Milosz. Used by permission of Doubleday, a division of Random House, Inc. "Lot's Wife" and "On the Banks of the Styx" from *View with a Grain of Sand*, copyright © 1993 by Wislawa Szymborska, English translation by Stanislaw Baranczak and Clare Cavanagh copyright © 1995 by Harcourt Brace & Company, reprinted by permission of the publisher.

Ingeborg Bachmann. "You want the summer lightening" and "The First-born Land," translated by Daniel Huws, and "Out of the corpse-warm vestibule . . .," translated by Janice Orion, appeared in *A Book of Women Poets from Antiquity to Now*, edited by Aliki Barnstone and Willis Barnstone (Schocken Books, 1980).

Anne Sexton. "Mary's Song" from *The Death Notebooks*. Copyright © 1974 by Anne Sexton. Reprinted by permission of Houghton Mifflin Company. All rights reserved. "As It Was Written" from *The Complete Poems of Anne Sexton*. Copyright © 1981 by Linda Gray Sexton and Loring Conant, Jr., executors of the will of Anne Sexton. Reprinted by permission of Houghton Mifflin Company. All rights reserved. "Not So. Not So." from *The Awful Rowing Toward God*. Copyright © 1975 by Loring Conant, Jr., executor of the Estate. Reprinted by permission of Houghton Mifflin Company. All rights reserved. "Somewhere in Africa" from *Live Or Die*. Copyright © 1966 by Anne Sexton. Reprinted by permission of Houghton Mifflin Company. All rights reserved.

Sylvia Plath. All lines from "Edge" from *Ariel* by Sylvia Plath. Copyright © 1963 by Ted Hughes. Copyright renewed. Reprinted by permission of HarperCollins Publishers, Inc., and Faber and Faber, Ltd. All lines from "Crossing the Water" from *Crossing the Water* by Sylvia Plath. Copyright © 1962 by Ted Hughes. Copyright renewed. Reprinted by permission of HarperCollins Publishers, Inc, and Faber and Faber, Ltd. All lines from "The Moon and the Yew Tree" from *The Collected Poems of Sylvia Plath*, edited by Ted Hughes. Copyright © 1963 by the Estate of Sylvia Plath. Copyright renewed. Reprinted by permission of HarperCollins Publishers, Inc., and Faber and Faber, Ltd.

Ingrid Jonker. "This Journey" translated by Jack Cope and William Plomer from *Selected Poems* by Ingrid Jonker, translated from the Afrikaans by Jack Cope and William Plomer. Reprinted by permission of the Estate of Ingrid Jonker and Jonathan Cape Ltd.

Lucille Clifton. "Leda 1" from *The Book of Light* © 1993 by Lucille Clifton. Reprinted by permission of Copper Canyon Press, Post Office Box 271, Port Townsend, WA 98368. "anna speaks of the childhood of mary her daughter" and "holy night," copyright © 1980 by Lucille Clifton. These poems now appear in *Good Woman*. Published by BOA Editions, Ltd. Reprinted by permission of Curtis Brown, Ltd. "slaveships," "david, musing," and "what manner of man" copyright © 1996 by Lucille Clifton. Reprinted from *The Terrible Stories* with permission of BOA Editions, Ltd., 260 East Ave., Rochester, NY 14604.

Bella Akhmadulina. "In the Emptied Rest Home" from *Poets on Street Corners* by Olga Carlisle. Copyright © 1968 by Random House, Inc. Reprinted by permission of Random House, Inc.

Linda Gregg. "Slow Dance by the Ocean," "In Dirt under Olive Trees on the Hill at Evening," "A Flower No More than Itself," and "All the Spring Lends Itself to Her" copyright 1991 by Linda Gregg. Reprinted from *The Sacraments of Desire* with the permission of Graywolf Press, Saint Paul, Minnesota. "God's Places" copyright 1994 by Linda Gregg. Reprinted from *Chosen by the Lion* with the permission of Graywolf Press, Saint Paul, Minnesota.

Jeni Couzyn. "Spell for Jealousy" and "Creation" from *The Heineman Book of African Women's Poetry*, edited by Stella and Frank Chipasula,